The opportunities of a lifetime

Model lifetime analysis of current British social policy

Martin Evans and Jill Eyre

T0335168

There are many here among us who feel that life is but a joke
But you and I, we've been through that, and this is not our fate.

(Bob Dylan, 'All along the Watchtower')

To Diamond and Jack

First published in Great Britain in November 2004 by

The Policy Press
Fourth Floor, Beacon House
Queen's Road
Bristol BS8 1QU
UK

Tel no   +44 (0)117 331 4054
Fax no   +44 (0)117 331 4093
E-mail   tpp-info@bristol.ac.uk
www.policypress.org.uk

© University of Bath 2004

Published for the Joseph Rowntree Foundation by The Policy Press

ISBN 1 86134 651 4

British Library Cataloguing in Publication Data
A catalogue record for this report is available from the British Library.

Library of Congress Cataloging-in-Publication Data
A catalog record for this report has been requested.

Martin Evans is a Senior Research Fellow and **Jill Eyre** is a Research Officer, both in the Centre for Analysis of Social Policy, Department of Social and Policy Sciences, University of Bath, UK.

All rights reserved: no part of this publication may be reproduced, stored in a retrieval system, or transmitted in any form or by any means, electronic, mechanical, photocopying, recording or otherwise without the prior written permission of the Publishers.

The **Joseph Rowntree Foundation** has supported this project as part of its programme of research and innovative development projects, which it hopes will be of value to policy makers, practitioners and service users. The facts presented and views expressed in this report are, however, those of the authors and not necessarily those of the Foundation.

The statements and opinions contained within this publication are solely those of the authors and not of The University of Bristol or The Policy Press. The University of Bristol and The Policy Press disclaim responsibility for any injury to persons or property resulting from any material published in this publication.

The Policy Press works to counter discrimination on grounds of gender, race, disability, age and sexuality.

Cover design by Qube Design Associates, Bristol
Front cover: photograph supplied by kind permission of www.JohnBirdsall.co.uk
Printed in Great Britain by Henry Ling Ltd, Dorchester

Contents

List of tables, figures and boxes

Tables

Figures

Boxes

Acknowledgements

The past 18 months have seen us take the germ of a rather mad and ambitious idea and bring it to reality. Thank you to everyone who said either, "You're trying to do what!.... Why?" or, "Well, it's obvious you should have used Access©".

The Joseph Rowntree Foundation has been everything one could ask for in terms of support and patience over the period, especially Anne Harrop, who shared our early ideas and saw their potential, and Chris Goulden, who has steered us through and been a supportive, kind and generous critic. Our advisory committee, Jane Millar, David Piachaud, Susan Harkness, Holly Sutherland, Richard Exell, Joanne Segars, Richard d'Souza, Clare Montagu, Charlie Pate and Mike Bielby, together with Rob James, Mario Pisani and Henry Bottomley, have all been constructive, insightful and generous friends of the project. A big thank you for the patience and interest of government modelling experts Jude Hilary, and the Pensim2 team, especially Ashwin Kumar, Jake McDonald, Matt Rudd and Clive Richardson.

We were also lucky to present early findings to a seminar in January 2004 where Mike Brewer, Helen John and Anne Bowtell were especially helpful. Our colleagues at Bath also helped with great questions, advice and appropriate gasps of amazement when we began showing results and running the programme. Unsung but essential technical help came from Rich Allen's brilliant programming skills and training from Steve Jones of Insight Computing. Both have been essential to the project. Also, a big thank you to the Child Poverty Action Group training department who taught us the workings of the modern benefit system. Last but foremost, to Flor and Simon who have had to live with our preoccupation with LOIS over the past year or so.

We acknowledge the copyright held on extracts from lyrics quoted: 'All along the watchtower' by Bob Dylan Copyright © 1968; renewed 1996 Dwarf Music; 'Know that' by Mos Def © Mos Def 2001 and 'The river' by Bruce Springsteen © Bruce Springsteen (ASCAP).

Of course, no one in this long list bears any responsibility for any mistakes or misinterpretations herein. They are ours alone. We also find ourselves in the unique position in a research report on social policy in having to make the following disclaimer:

The events and characters depicted in this report are fictitious. Any similarity to actual persons, living or dead is purely coincidental. However, resonance with readers' concerns for their own lives and/or the lives of their friends or loved ones is intended and welcome.

Social policy, life chances and the lifetime

> [Beveridge] advocated something not yet attempted before:
> not just a universal embrace for one branch of social policy
> or another, but a comprehensive, complete system... (Baldwin, 1994, p 45)

Social policy has a history of advocates who approached policy from a lifetime perspective. In the early years of the 20th century, Seebohm Rowntree described how the lifetime income profile produced high risks and incidence of poverty in childhood and old age (Rowntree, 1902). Interest has resurfaced since the 1990s, with a surge of analysis of lifetime social policy, mostly in response to questions about pension policy, caring for higher numbers of older people with greater needs and the impact of childhood and education on the lifetime. Much of this has been driven by a growing stock of data from birth cohort studies that began in the 1950s and 1970s and from panel data that began in the early 1990s. Policy analysts have thus developed descriptive, analytical and predictive techniques that take lifetime impacts into account.

Policy makers also view the life course as important; most efforts have been to recognise the developmental needs and approaches in child development and youth policy, such as SureStart and Connexions and the New Deal for Young People respectively, or for the end of the life course when designing pensions and considering long-term care issues for older people. Policy makers in recent years have not looked much *across* various policy interventions to assess consistency and comprehensiveness of a lifetime design. The 1942 Beveridge Report had such an approach. Recent reforms since 1997 do sum up to a package that can be seen as covering the life course and have been described by the Prime Minister as "more ambitious and far-reaching than any since the Second World War" (DSS, 1998, p iii). If it is true that we have reached another epochal moment in the British welfare state, it is opportune to take stock and see how lifetime needs and security are designed into the current system – is there a lifetime vision to match Beveridge's vision of comprehensive coverage for all citizens, 'from the cradle to the grave'?

An idea of a lifetime is central to who we are. We rarely think of ourselves purely in the present. We look forward and back to assess where we are in our life course and to compare ourselves to our parents, peers and children. Our opportunities usually seem richer than those of our parents' generation, while we hope our children will take on the opportunities we missed in our lives and avoid our pitfalls. Lifetimes do not always hold a clear or positive narrative. Many people do not have an overall lifetime vision and wish they did. The life course also has risks, dead-ends and disappointments. Evidence of frustrated and blighted lives comes daily from newspapers and the television, in contrast to bookshops' bulging shelves of biographies to admire and inspire. Lifetimes, whether positive or negative, have thus great potential and resonance to inform us about our society and ourselves and our lifetime identity is precious.

Aims of the report

We have three main aims:

- to describe the current system in an accessible manner to a wide audience and to illustrate how the system performs using lifetime profiles;
- to analyse the current system and its potential coverage over the lifetime and how it responds to opportunities and risks;
- to provide a form of systemic health check and alert policy makers and others to potential weaknesses of the current system to lifetime profiles of risk and opportunities.

Our concern to inform springs in part from the extreme complexity of the current system. There are now different means tests across benefits for those out of work, in work and pensioner groups, for instance. Also, the interaction of the state system with private forms of investment and savings is now potentially very complex. While there has been a large increase in the volume of information available to help us – on the web, from financial advisers and from government leaflets and policy documents – such information tends to be specific to a particular benefit programme, private financial service, risk and point in time. Two common problems are thus independence and comprehensiveness. Independent, value-free information is also rare as consumer-orientated advertising, press bias and political spin and rhetoric make sorting fact from opinion or hard-sell a continual stressful task. Information is partial in both meanings of the term. Those we trust and respect have limited knowledge: our peers are in the same boat, our elders lived under a different system and our children may not be in the position to assist in funding our pensions as we currently fund our parents'. Our children are also too precious to allow calculations based on individual risk to completely influence our actions today – can I make my child poor now because I want to assure that I will not be poor when I retire?

But integrated comprehensive information is also rare. If, say, we want to know about paying into a pension alongside having children, there is no ability to join together what any information provider provides. But this is a very common need during our lives today. How do we add up the risks, make choices and plan our lives? While this report can never answer every reader's particular questions, it does aim to provide a series of lifetime road maps through the complex jungle of information and rules.

Our aim to analyse springs from a need to join up all the change from recent policy developments and see how they stand when taken together. Society and the economy have changed hugely since the 1980s, let alone since the Beveridge Report, and the assumptions behind social policy have changed at the same time. The mixture of state benefits, tax credits, and private and occupational pensions alongside taxes, National Insurance payments and private saving make it necessary to gauge their potential combined impact and to assess both short- and long-term effects on life chances. Individuals are expected to engage fully with the complex system in order to take responsibility for planning their financial security and to invest in underlying educational levels and skills. This increased emphasis on individual responsibility has occurred, in part, because the government has stepped back from universal strategies of pooling risk across the whole population when faced with increased uncertainty and its potential costs. However, the image of 'stepping back' is ambivalent because in many ways the government has also stepped forward – making investment in pensions more regulated, as well as 'simpler' and more cost-effective for those on lower incomes. It has also stepped forward in other ways: encouraging employment through a huge investment in the New Deals; helping improve parental employment through childcare and greater parental rights at work; and developing a more comprehensive system of in-work Income Support. It has also encouraged greater enrolment in higher education and to increasing skills of the workforce. Understanding the impact of these changes and their potential influence on our life chances is understandably difficult.

The new policy mix is also more difficult to envisage as a single system akin to Beveridge's concept of 'social security' because we now have fragmentation of various tax credits, benefits, statutory pay provisions alongside occupational and private pensions. Both private and state means-tested provision have grown in importance as contributory social insurance has declined. What was 'social security' has been spread across the Department for Work and Pensions and the Inland Revenue, which now operate all the tax credits alongside tax and National Insurance contributions. Nevertheless, we still call the current overall system by the term 'social security', as using anything else ends up an inelegant list of programmes and initiatives.

How does this current system of 'social security' work and what are its outcomes for people with different income levels and circumstances over their lifetimes? Our systematic and strategic analysis means bringing together:

- the *whole* system of taxes, benefits and related policy instruments that affect our education, work, retirement and family life;
- *our lifetimes*, to reflect on both now, the next few years and the longer future potential of social security to assist with our education during our working lives, when we have children, and in our retirement.

So, 62 years on from the Beveridge Report, how does the new system provide security and support opportunity over the lifetime?

Our aim to be evaluative is cautious and particular. It rests on a particular method of analysis described more fully below. Basically, we simulate the effect of everyone living their whole lives under the current system – an impossibility in practice but the only way of assessing how current policy design and rules add up in their treatment of children, working adults and pensioners together. The strength of this approach is that it takes all the policy makers' assumptions and joins them together. But many of these assumptions may have been made without thinking that they would or could be so joined. Some decisions may have been made with only short-term consequences in mind – to solve a particular problem today and without reference to a far-away future. Indeed, some decisions are deliberately kept to 'the lifetime of this Parliament' so as not to commit future policy makers. If this is the case then we inevitably illustrate the shortcomings of short-termism but do so without party political or adversarial intent. Our approach is one of a neutral 'critical friend'. Our analysis finds *potential* policy failings and identifies future unsustainability, and such results will no doubt be taken by some as ammunition for an anti-government or party political argument. Our intention is more strategic and informative; to stand above the short-term political cycle and show the consequences of current policy assumptions and approaches. These are shared across a very wide spectrum of political actors and cannot be solely laid at the present government's door. Furthermore, we do not attempt to formulate or assess alternatives to current policy. That is a bigger and more ambitious project.

The research approach

Our analysis uses a custom-built lifetime simulation model that can calculate entitlement to all aspects of social security under any hypothetical lifetime lived under the current (2003/04) policy regime. This means that, from the age of 16, a whole range of behaviour can be simulated in education and work, in partnering and having children, in savings and pension uptake and in retirement. Earnings histories of different sorts can be compared alongside experience of different risks and opportunities. We have named our simulation model LOIS, the *Lifetime Opportunities and Incentives Simulation*. LOIS calculates all taxes, tax credits, benefits, private and occupational pensions, savings and can report on how income changes over the lifetime – both in its components and in their combined level when measured alongside poverty. Fuller details of LOIS and how to contact the researchers are contained in the Appendix. LOIS can thus recreate profiles used by Seebohm Rowntree some 100 years ago and look at periods of relative security and insecurity over the lifetime. Additionally, LOIS can also report on the constraints on taking opportunities over the lifetime – the effective marginal tax rates from working more as well as the long-term benefits or disbenefits of working longer, saving and owning a home, for instance.

Our approach is unique and innovative and allows a strategic analysis of how the current social security system comes together. Others have used similar approaches to simulation but usually only of parts of the social security system – pensions in particular – or for specific social and economic concerns such as women's lifetimes. **Box 1.1** gives an overview of policy simulation and lifetime simulation and explains where our approach fits alongside other research.

Our aim is to bench-test the current policy regime in a similar way to how engineers and architects place aeroplanes and buildings in a wind tunnel to see how the design performs under simulated climatic conditions. Our bench test uses simulated lifetimes to see how the various elements of policy interact and how outcomes arise and cumulate over the lifetime alongside inflation. This approach tells us much about the sustainability and sense of current policy design over the medium- to long-term as well as how far the government's approach to the life course is 'joined up'. This main focus on policy design leads us to look at three core questions:

- What packages of income assistance do people get as they progress through their lifetime?
- How do these packages protect against income poverty?
- What are the resulting opportunities, incentives and risks and how do these change and interact with different work, individual and family histories?

To answer these questions we construct and follow several model lifetimes lived entirely under the current social policy regime. These lifetimes are 'hypothetical' – they are not actual people and there are no underlying data from surveys or other sources that directly give rise to their lifetime circumstances. This means that the lifetime circumstances are not empirical and should not be treated as such. They are illustrative and are chosen to closely relate to present-day circumstances and be indicative of the risks and opportunities we all face.

The model lifetimes are thus not the 'real world' and, because LOIS simulations use the actual policy rules in current legislation, this also means that the policy world over the lifetime is not 'real'. In reality, policy changes as we grow older as politicians incrementally change programmes. LOIS instead freezes today's rules of entitlement to benefits and liabilities for taxes and today's pensions and education grants and other policy programmes. Why then create a world where policy is held constant?

- It enables an analysis of overall policy design that can ignore rules for 'transitional' protection that are there to protect people who could lose entitlement when policy is changed.
- It enables us to focus on the way that policy treats different risks and periods of the lifetime by holding everything else constant.
- It enables us to look at the assumptions about inflation and up-rating of policy elements.

Box 1.1: Policy simulation and the lifetime

Simulation and modelling are standard methods of policy analysis – summarising key elements of the system as they apply to individuals and families in a comprehensive way and using the models to examine the outcomes (for example, in income levels or poverty rates) for different combinations and levels of inputs. The annual series of Department for Work and Pensions (DWP) Tax Benefit Model Tables provides summary tables for specified family types, showing the taxes and benefits paid and received for gross earnings between £0 and about £900 per week (for example, DWP, 2003a). These are used to calculate replacement ratios (income in work relative to income out of work) and effective marginal tax rates (the level of deductions for each additional £ earned) for the specified family types. One way of conceptualising LOIS is to think of this approach undertaken for every quarter in a lifetime rather than for each additional amount of earnings for a cross-sectional case.

Jonathan Bradshaw and his colleagues at the University of York have developed this sort of methodology in the form of 'model family' cross-national comparisons of support for children (Bradshaw et al, 1993, 1996; Bradshaw and Finch, 2002), of social assistance (Eardley et al, 1996a, 1996b), and of support for lone parents and families more generally (Kilkey, 2000). As they point out, the advantages of this 'model family' approach are that it enables comparisons to be made on a like-by-like basis and controls for elements of variation between countries by holding a set of family composition and employment circumstances constant (see discussion in Bradshaw and Finch, 2002).

Alongside a model family approach is micro-simulation modelling, which can examine the distribution of policy outcomes in the population by simulating tax/benefit rules to an actual sample of the population to assess the impact of policy and changes in policy. Holly Sutherland's 'Polimod' and 'Euromod' and the Institute for Fiscal Studies/HM Treasury Inter Governmental Tax and Benefit Model (IGOTM) models are examples of this approach, with Euromod providing the opportunity for cross-national comparisons (Redmond et al, 1998, provide a good overview of micro-simulation approaches).

These sorts of models, both the model family and cross-sectional micro-simulation models, provide a snapshot of the impact of the tax/benefit regime and are thus static, in the sense that they examine outcomes for individuals and families at one point in their lives. They model the outcome as it would happen now, that is, in terms of current income or current poverty or current marginal tax rates, and so on. This is only a partial picture, since the tax/benefit regime has an impact on longer-term, as well as current, income. Dynamic micro-simulation has evolved to simulate policy outcomes over a lifetime or other dynamic longitudinal perspective. Development of such models has been led by pension simulation and other issues that reflect the interaction of people's employment and demographic histories. Dynamic simulation is stochastic in approach, reflecting underlying probabilities of lifetime events and trajectories on the underlying population. Our approach to lifetime simulation is different. We take forward and expand the 'model family' approach to enable a wide variety of model lifetimes with which to profile policy systems using non-static but constant sets of lifetime circumstances for individuals and their partners and children (if any) over a simulated lifetime. This approach follows a small, but growing, literature on hypothetical life course modelling. These studies have analysed the long-term outcomes of particular patterns of lifetime employment and earnings on incomes (Joshi et al, 1996, and Rake, 2000 employ this method to look at women's lifetimes incomes), or to look at pension design (Evans and Falkingham, 1997; Evans et al, 1999; Rake et al, 2000). Johnson has also used a variant of this approach to look comparatively at pension developments in Europe since the 1950s (Johnson, 1999).

Holding policy constant over a lifetime thus enables us to take policy makers' assumptions about now and the future and join them up. The approach allows us to emulate the perspective of a modern-day Beveridge – to stand back and assess how social security provides and protects us from the cradle to the grave.

Reading and using the report

This report is written for a variety of audiences and purposes. The central unifying theme is the lifetime and the whole report is based around describing and analysing a series of lifetimes. Particular elements of social security such as pensions, benefits for children, higher education loans, in-work benefits and other areas are integrated into the lifetime approach. At the same time, the report unfolds from a simplified single lifetime on average earnings in which pensions are the prominent lifetime policy problem, to low-paid lifetimes families with children, and then to lifetime risk events. This means that readers interested in particular areas of policy can dip selectively into the right place in the report. Additionally, we cover the main policy areas in the conclusion to place the potential lessons from the analysis in their respective policy-making silos.

By concentrating the story on the lifetimes, we hope to take a more policy-hesitant reader through the issues without all of the technical and system-specific detail that complicates and obscures so much debate about social security. This means that readers who want only to get the main arguments can read the lifetime stories and their outcomes and then the conclusions. Text boxes provide more details of how the system works and of the simulations and methodology that we have undertaken and these are placed throughout the chapters. At the same time, we aim to build up the complexities of lifetime analysis as the report progresses. Our first model lifetimes are the simplest and have very basic assumptions about earnings growth and other lifetime events. By Chapter 5 we have introduced more complex approaches using age-related earnings profiles and also introducing lifetime events alongside simple lifetime trajectories.

Our series of model lifetimes thus builds cumulatively to provide an analysis of today's social security and tax system. Each model lifetime is highly simplified and stereotypical in order to illustrate and explain the policy structures and policy dilemmas that arise over the lifetime. However, we base profiles on evidence where possible, as there is a lot of longitudinal and other evidence to inform us of incomes, family formation and economic risks over the lifetime. Longitudinal evidence can sometimes be of limited value because the birth cohorts from the late 1950s and 1970s have not yet lived full lifetimes and started in very different social, economic and policy environments, but still provides a huge source of evidence on changing behaviour over the lifetime since the mid-20th century[1]. The British Household Panel Study, which has followed a cross-section of the population since 1992, is additionally helpful to assist in understanding a variety of lifetime events and risks across the population profile over the past 11 years.

Each of our model lifetimes is given a name and thus relates to a fictional individual.

- Chapter 2: *Mr Modal* has average earnings but remains single all his life. His twin sister *Ms Modal* has average female earnings and is described to show the issues of gender-based pay and life expectancy. The main policy area discussed is pension provision.
- Chapter 3, describing *Mr Meager*, focuses on the issue of low pay. It explores how a low-paid lifetime potentially differs from *Mr Modal's* and what can be done to improve *Mr Meager's* life chances. The main policy area discussed is pension provision.

---

[1] ESRC (2004) provides a good starting point for consideration of this evidence.

Box 1.2: LOIS simulations: basic lifetime assumptions

Macro-economy
- Both earnings and price inflation are constant over the lifetime, with no cyclical variations of 'boom or bust'.
- The underlying inflation rates are set at those used by the government in the Green Paper on Pensions (DWP, 2002):
  - 2.5% per annum for prices;
  - 4.55% per annum for earnings (a real rate of earnings growth of 2.05%);
  - inflation rates can differ for housing costs (house prices, rents), Council Tax and childcare.
- Investment growth:
  - 4% per annum for savings account;
  - 6.5% per annum for pension fund growth;
  - 4.5% per annum for annuity rates.

Lifetimes and life events
- All hypothetical people are single generation simulations that begin at age 16 in April 2003 and are based around a single named individual.
- Partners and children are attached to this individual and then detached as appropriate to reflect leaving home and separation.
- Income and events are simulated every quarter. This allows periods during the lifetime to be a minimum of 13 weeks. This leads to rounding in certain benefit entitlements such as Maternity Pay, which is paid at different rates for six-week periods.

Consistent definitions for this report
To keep lifetimes simple for discussion we have adopted the following conventions for this report.

- All begin at 16 and all individuals are born on the same day. This means that partners are of exactly the same age.
- Partners' circumstances are not simulated after the death of the named model lifetime in this report and there is thus no discussion of survivorship.
- We have harmonised life expectancy for all simulated lives in this report at the age of 81. This is to enable simple consistent comparisons to be made that can change for all other events and trajectories apart from longevity.

- Chapter 4 focuses on couples with children and how children alter lifetime earnings and policy profiles. *The Middletons* have average earnings and *The Lowes* are low paid. Both these families have identical lives but take forward the previous examples of *Mr Modal* and *Mr Meager*. How can changing earnings profiles and childcare arrangements help reduce different lifetime outcomes for these families? The main policy interactions discussed are children's benefits, part-time working and childcare.
- Chapter 5 focuses on three major risks over the lifetime and each therefore represents both a policy focus and a model lifetime: *Mr Jobin* who experiences unemployment, *Mr Hales* who has sickness and a disablement that renders him incapable of work in his later life and *Ms Singleton* who experiences lone parenthood. The three lifetimes explored are, apart from the risk events, identical to *Mr Meager* and to *The Lowes* from Chapters 3 and 4.
- Last, Chapter 6 takes all the analysis gained from these lifetimes and discusses the cumulative findings of this analysis and how they relate to the real policy world. What have they shown us about the current policy regime and how could some of the apparent policy problems we have identified be resolved?

More details of the LOIS simulation model are in the Appendix and can be seen at www.lois-web.org

Model lifetimes and an average life

Next to knowing when to seize an opportunity;
the most important thing in life is
knowing when to forgo an advantage. (Disraeli)

This chapter introduces the current tax and benefit system and its lifetime simulation through a hypothetical character called *Mr Modal*.

Mr Modal

Mr Modal lives up to his name by having characteristics associated with an 'average' lifetime and is, in essence, a simple benchmark 'model lifetime'. But an average lifetime is a slippery concept as the sequencing and mix of events and trajectories are not understandable as averages. Current cross-sectional data gives us much information about the current population but is based on a specific age composition. There are the most common ages at which events occur – leaving the parental home, getting a first job, getting married, having children and retirement, for instance. Cumulating these modal ages together, however, gives rise to a nonsensical lifetime and we act carefully to ensure that events and profiles match current empirical evidence in a coherent way. Mr Modal represents a man's lifetime precisely because we wish to discuss gender penalties on employment, having children, caring for children and women's earnings profiles more fully later, both in this chapter and in Chapter 4.

Mr Modal's lifetime story begins at the age of 16 with continuing his education in school or college and then taking a degree. Taking up higher education is not currently average behaviour for young people, but with a stated government aim to increase participation rates to 50%, it is a reasonable modal assumption to make about the future. Mr Modal thus starts work at the age of 21. He remains single throughout his life, never ceases working or has any interruptions to work due to unemployment or sickness. He retires at the age of 65, and has a current average life expectancy for a man of that age and thus dies aged 81 (GAD, 2003). While this is a fairly simple life, there are several elements that need careful explanation.

Mr Modal has average earnings, which at 2003 figures from the New Earnings Survey are £489 per week (roughly £25,450 per annum). However, what are average earnings over a lifetime when earnings potentially change over the working life due to experience, relative value of human capital to the employer and other factors. In this chapter we keep our earnings profile very simple and use nominal average earnings inflated on a constant assumption of earnings inflation over the whole working life. This is not to be 'realistic' but reflects more realistic expectations of the amount of variations and events that can be put

Box 2.1: Earnings profiles over the lifetime

In this chapter we keep earnings growing linearly by average earnings growth over the lifetime for the sake of simplicity and ease of interpretation at 4.55% every year in line with the underlying assumptions about average earnings growth used by the government when discussing pension provision. In later chapters we use different earnings assumptions. The earnings profile from 16 until retirement is the most important element in lifetime simulations of taxes and benefits. There are several choices in approaches and methods:

- *Earnings inflation with no earnings progression:* this earnings profile allows an 'average' or other benchmark wage level to be imputed over the whole working lifetime with no variation for age or for changing jobs or gaining experience. This is the simplest assumption and is used throughout this report as a way of producing easily interpretable results and is the sole method in this chapter.
- *Age-related earnings profile:* earnings levels differ over the working life – starting low as experience is gained and then peaking in the person's forties and then levelling off in later years. Current cross-sectional age profiles from the New Earnings Survey are used to produce such a profile. However, differences in composition of the workforce, particularly differential rates of early retirement between higher and lower earners in later life, will understate earnings for older workers and thus overstate decreases in earnings for older workers in an age-related profile. This method is used in Chapter 5 to show the importance of timing of risks in the lifetime.
- *Customised earnings to simulate progression:* this is used in Chapter 3 to show the effects of raising earnings through earnings progression (promotion, job mobility, and so on).

Figure 2.1 shows examples of each of these three types of earnings profiles: a simple linear inflated average, a basic age-related profile and a customised linear average with earnings progression (5% every four years from the age of 25 to 50).

- *Predicted earnings:* real data from the British Household Panel Survey can be used to create an earnings equation that can predict the earnings level based on individual characteristics and work history. This method is not used in this report but is available in LOIS. There is some underlying uncertainty about how robust predicted earnings will be if the set of circumstances used are not common in the underlying survey data.

All earnings profiles are based on hourly rates of pay and our basic assumption is to use a standard working week of 38 hours. This means that in fact the product of average hourly pay at 38 hours a week does not match average earnings levels. However, using 38 hours a week as a standard assumption for full-time work allows us to easily show the effect of working an additional hour when calculating and discussing marginal tax rates (see Chapter 4 for discussion).

forward in this first chapter of the report. The report's approach becomes more complicated as we progress and readers follow the cumulative building up of lifetime profiles and events. **Box 2.1** shows the assumptions and methodology for using different ways of estimating earnings over the working life and LOIS' options for doing so.

Mr Modal's lifetime financial profile additionally relates to his investment behaviour alongside his income. At 18 we have allowed for his Child Trust Fund to mature, and we have allowed him to spend this in full, perhaps during his university years to pay for a variety of things during his studies. In our simple case, he thus begins his working life with no savings but a debt from his student loan. Current legislation before Parliament will raise such debts for future graduates, but we base our case on an outstanding student loan

Figure 2.1: Lifetime earnings profiles: indexed average, age related and earnings progression assumptions

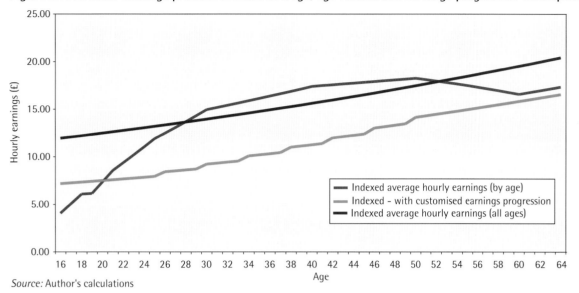

Source: Author's calculations

based on figures for the current average of £7,300[2] (DfES, 2004). It is sensible to assume that repayment of debt will delay Mr Modal's other investment decisions, so we make his investment decisions sequential so that he delays saving towards buying a house until he has paid off his student loan, and then saves around a 10% deposit towards a home. In the meantime we assume that while he is paying back his student loan and building up his savings he rents his home. At average earnings this means that it will take him until he is 33 to save the deposit for an average-priced home for a first-time buyer (currently £127,389[3]). Of course, while our Mr Modal's lifetime employs a single generation assumption, in reality it is highly likely that he would receive help towards his house purchase from his parents or even grandparents or other relative[4].

During the period when he moves into his home and repays his loan, we assume a stable macro-economic environment in which interest rates remain constant over the period of his mortgage. We also assume, for the sake of simplicity, that he lives in this house for the remainder of his life rather than trading up and/or down later in his life cycle. Even so, this very simple housing career contains some assumptions about house price inflation and affordability that are explained in **Box 2.2**.

The other major investment decision that Mr Modal would have to make during his working life concerns pensions. This is an issue that we put to one side for the moment and return to later in this chapter, but let us in the first instance assume that he makes no decision about pensions other than to pay his National Insurance contributions (NICs) and to solely receive state pensions.

---

2   The DfES report an average overall student debt of £8,666, of which 84% (£7,279) is from student loans.

3   ODPM Statistical Release March 2004 (HPI-3-04 Table A4), price at January 2004 for first-time buyers.

4   See the MORI report for the Joseph Rowntree Foundation (2004).

Box 2.2: House prices, incomes and affordability

Long-term rising house prices exemplify the British housing market's post-war performance. However, recent increases since the late 1990s have been particularly high. What level can house prices rise over the lifetime? When we look back to house prices 50 years ago, the average price in 1952 was just over £2,000 and house prices have risen on average at around 8.5% per annum. If we take a shorter, more recent period, from 1991 to 2003, then house prices have risen at around 7.5% per annum.

The problem with these historical price trends is that they are far higher than the government's assumptions about earnings growth over the next 50 years – 4.55%. Such trends over time would make home ownership unaffordable to a wider band of earners. The current average earnings to average price ratio for such a first-time purchase is 5:1. With recent house price inflation trends of 7.5% per annum this ratio would rise to 7.8:1 over 16 years.

We use a house price inflation figure of 6% per annum – slightly over earnings inflation – in all simulations. This raises the affordability ratio from 5:1 to 6.2:1 for Mr Modal by the time he purchases at age 33. We also simulate saving for a 10% deposit towards his purchase from the point at which he has paid off his student loan (aged 24¾). To be able to save sufficient funds for a 10% deposit on a home we have calculated that savings levels would be £75 a week (£3,900 a year) with a savings account interest rate of 4.25% and taking advantage of full ISA tax free saving limits a year (£3,000 in 2003/04 policy rules). This provides Mr Modal with a deposit of just over £40,000.

Mr Modal's lifetime income profile

Figure 2.2 shows the income components and profile for Mr Modal's lifetime using these assumptions about income, tenure and investment. All income sources are shown as a percentage of average earnings in gross amounts while taxes, national insurance payments and student loan repayments are shown as negative amounts. The largest element of income over Mr Modal's lifetime is his earnings, which appears flat overall from the age of 21 to 65. The other source of income shown during the working years is the interest paid

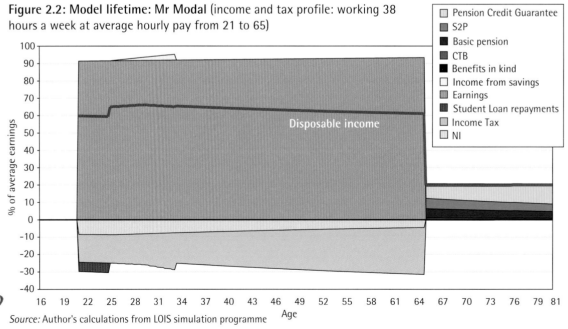

Figure 2.2: Model lifetime: Mr Modal (income and tax profile: working 38 hours a week at average hourly pay from 21 to 65)

Source: Author's calculations from LOIS simulation programme

Box 2.3: Up-rating

Up-rating of benefits and taxes is an issue that lies at the core of politics and policy making. Too often political ideas are seen as the most fundamental aspect of policy making, but in reality the continuing political process has an equal if not more important effect. There are basically four choices for up-rating: not to bother, to up-rate with price inflation to up-rate with earnings or to duck the issue and tinker as one needs to over time. We can simulate the first three.

- Maintaining nominal amounts: not bothering with up-rating occurs frequently across fiscal policy and many elements of the current tax benefit system have remained unchanged for many years. The savings thresholds for means-tested benefits is an obvious choice – the lower level of £3,000 has remained constant since 1988, similarly income disregards for means-tested benefits, the extra pension given to the over eighties (25p a week), and savings levels for tax exemption (ISAs for instance) are all set at nominal amounts with no commitments to up-rate.
- Up-rating with price inflation is a central element of most benefit legislation and, in theory, protects the purchasing power of benefits.
- Up-rating with earnings protects incomes as a relative standard and used to be the norm in the 1960s and 1970s. Harold Macmillan made a great play of raising National Assistance (the old scheme of what is now called Income Support) in the early 1960s to allow the poorest to share in growing national wealth. However, such a 'One Nation' approach ended in 1982 when benefits and pensions were changed to be up-rated with prices. As we will see later in this chapter, this has had a marked effect on the relative value of the State Retirement Pension but has affected all benefits. Politically this is a less obvious strategy to cut spending over time and lowers the risk of identifiable 'losers'. But the much criticised inflation rise of only 75p for pensions in the recent past marks an embarrassing example of how politically sensitive up-rating policy can be if it allows relative income standards to fall noticeably.

Recently there has been a limited re-emergence of commitments to earnings up-rating – for some elements of Child Tax Credit over the lifetime of the Parliament and for Pension Credit in the future.

Over the medium to long term, a policy of no up-rating or of up-rating with price inflation can be unsustainable and what occurs are periodic reviews that actually lead to a ratchet effect, and the fourth stated option for up-rating. Such an approach is difficult to simulate and our assumptions in this report are to show the effects of *current practice or of currently stated commitments* on up-rating.

on the savings that Mr Modal builds up while saving for the deposit on his home purchase (see the discussion in **Box 2.2**).

Looking below the zero line of the *X*-axis of **Figure 2.2** at student loan repayments, taxes and national insurance contributions, we see that for the first three and three quarter years Mr Modal is paying a considerable portion of his earnings in these forms of taxation and loan repayments – about 30%. After student loan repayments end, the profile of tax payments rises as a proportion of earnings. Why is this?

This effect springs from an assumption that tax thresholds (the income levels at which tax rates apply or end) rise with prices over a period when earnings are rising faster than prices. The difference means that higher proportions of income are taken in tax as earnings rise and overtake tax band thresholds and as Mr Modal ages his earnings fall more and more in the top tax bracket of 40%. This phenomenon is called 'fiscal drag'. **Box 2.3** outlines the main issues concerning up-rating of taxes and benefits and describes the underlying approach to our lifetime simulations.

Box 2.4: Income Tax and National Insurance contributions and up-rating

Table 2.1 gives the thresholds and rates of Income Tax and NICs for 2003/04.

The effect of current up-rating assumptions and practice on lifetime tax and NICs liability is dramatic. Figure 2.3 shows today's thresholds and earnings limits in real prices (adjusted for price inflation) and shows how continuing to up-rate these thresholds by price inflation while earnings rise faster is unsustainable and leads to average earnings falling within 40% tax bands and above the upper earning's limit within 10 years and the minimum wage falling in 40% tax bands over the lifetime.

Table 2.1: Income Tax and National Insurance 2003/04

Income Tax personal allowances	£ per week	Income Tax rates and thresholds below personal allowance	0%
Aged under 65	89	1st band up to £37.99	10%
Aged 65 to 74 (subject to income test)	127	2nd band £38-£587	22%
Aged 75 and over (subject to income test)	129	3rd band >£587	40%
NICs earnings thresholds 2003/04		NIC rates and credits	
LEL	77	Below LEL	No NICs/credits
Earnings threshold	89	LEL to PT	Credits given
UEL	595	LEL to UEL	11%
		Over UEL	1%

Notes: LEL = lower earnings limit
PT = primary threshold
UEL = upper earnings limit

Figure 2.3: Tax and National Insurance thresholds and average and minimum wages over the lifetime (real prices on current assumptions)

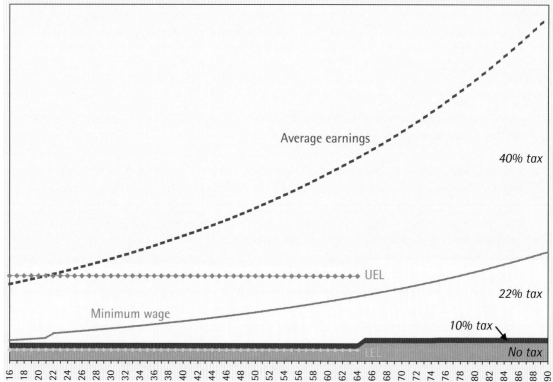

Tax and National Insurance

Income tax is payable on taxable income (earnings, interest from savings, pensions and *some* benefits) over the whole lifetime. NICs are payable on earnings up to the age of 65. Both Income Tax and NICs allow people to keep some level of income before they have to pay. These are called tax allowances for Income Tax, and are called the lower earnings limit (LEL) for NICs. The amount of tax increases as earnings rise (*progressivity*) and there are three rates of tax – 10%, 22% and 40%. NICs are less progressive and have an upper earnings limit (UEL) above which only 1% of earnings is paid. The current rates and thresholds for taxes and NICs are shown in **Box 2.4**, which also shows the effect of up-rating over the lifetime and discusses the long-term policy implications of fiscal drag.

These long-term profiles of tax and NI payments match current practice and stated policy commitments to changing these elements in the Budget and annual spending reviews. But it is arguable that such decisions are purely short-term ones that reflect concern with the contemporary state of public finances. Even so, the extent to which such short-term practice is sustainable in the medium to long term is an important one. In the short term, the government gains more revenue by allowing taxation thresholds to rise more slowly than earnings but the long-term implications for fiscal structures and interactions of taxes and benefits and with private investments are serious (see **Box 2.4**).

Turning to look at Mr Modal's retirement income, the large fall in relative income is obvious in **Figure 2.2** at the age of 65. He has made no provisions for his own retirement and relies on state benefits. Governments since 1982 have committed the basic state retirement pension to rise only with prices and the effect for Mr Modal is stark. His basic pension represents only 8% of average earnings. State Second Pension (S2P) paid in addition is around 6% of earnings at retirement, but the combination of basic pension and S2P is not enough to raise income above Pension Credit (Basic Guarantee) levels. Mr Modal therefore gets Pension Credit Guarantee as a top-up to his income to 20% of average earnings.

Mr Modal and lifetime poverty

How far does this lifetime income profile protect Mr Modal against poverty? The measurement of poverty is a complex area for policy analysis and gives rise to a number of approaches and standards. **Box 2.5** discusses these approaches and gives an overview of the calculations that we have used in this report. We employ a consistent poverty measure over the lifetime and need to compare the effect of benefits and tenure of a variety of lifetimes. The measure we use is thus the one adopted by the DWP in reporting poverty as income after housing costs (AHC) and based on 60% of median equivalent income. **Figure 2.4** shows Mr Modal's lifetime poverty profile. This shows how his net income after taxes, student loan repayments and housing costs (in this instance, the rent he pays until he is 33 and the interest he pays on his mortgage afterwards until he is 59 on a 25-year mortgage) compares to the poverty line over his whole lifetime.

Figure 2.4's lifetime profile for Mr Modal starts at the age of 21 when he ceases to be a student, enters the labour market and lives independently[5]. Mr Modal lives all his life above the poverty line and thus achieves consistent lifetime *poverty clearance*. His earnings after tax, National Insurance and student loan repayments from the ages of 21 to 24¾ give a

---

5 We have not attempted to estimate living standards while he is a student – there are many uncertainties about part-time and seasonal employment, parental contributions and other sources of income that make such estimation very uncertain.

Box 2.5: Poverty

There are several ways of measuring poverty. We conform to the methods used by the Households Below Average Income series, with some adaptations (DWP, 2004). The relative income poverty line takes 60% of median equivalised income as a standard. Income is equivalised in order to adjust it to household size and composition using scales that vary according to the number of adults and the number and age of children (see the discussion of equivalence scales below). The effect of equivalisation is that households can be ranked in income terms, holding the number and ages of household members constant. There are two main income definitions used to create a poverty line:

Before housing costs (BHC): this measures net income from all sources (earnings, self-employment, contributory and non-contributory benefits including Housing and Council Tax Benefits, tax credits, pensions, savings, maintenance, education grants and loans, and benefits in kind) after tax, NICs, Council Tax, contributions to private and occupational pensions, payments of maintenance and child support and parental payments to students living away from home.

After housing costs (AHC): this deducts the following housing costs from BHC-defined income: rent (total before Housing Benefit), water and sewerage charges, mortgage interest payments, buildings insurance and ground rent and leasehold service charges.

We have adapted these definitions to take into account the following:

Childcare costs are deducted from the BHC definition (and thus AHC) to reflect the fact that Working Tax Credit now gives assistance with childcare that would distort BHC income if underlying childcare costs were not also deducted.

Student loan repayments are deducted from the BHC definition to consistently treat higher education finance-related income and liabilities – such repayments are akin to a graduate tax and balance loan income included in the BHC measure earlier in the lifetime.

Extra cost disability benefits (Disability Living Allowance and Attendance Allowance) are not included in BHC income definitions as a way of equivalising income to take account of the needs of disability. This is discussed in greater detail in Box 5.3.

It should be noted that our calculations are set to Households Below Average Income (HBAI) 2001 levels (DWP, 2003b), the latest available figures at the point of undertaking all the analysis. Poverty lines were inflated using previous rises in median equivalent income to 2003/04 estimates. Our adaptations have not been used to recalculate the overall population median income level and poverty line. We continue to use the AHC poverty line from 2001 and this means that there is not an exact correspondence with published poverty standards. This is of most impact in model lifetimes that involve disability.

Income measure and equivalent scale adopted for the analysis

We use the AHC income measure and the McClements Scale AHC equivalence scale. This is consistent with the HBAI series but not consistent with DWP child poverty target definitions that use BHC income and OECD (Organisation for Economic Co-operation and Development) equivalence scales as their primary measure of relative poverty (DWP, 2003c). Our choice of equivalence scales reflected the absence of HBAI data on an OECD basis at the point of analysis and a preference for data that reflected established time series. Our choice of AHC income measure also reflects the need to consistently compare income over the lifetime between those renting and purchasing their homes and to properly take into account Housing Benefit income.

Poverty gaps and poverty clearance

Incomes below the poverty line have a poverty gap – the shortfall – measured as a percentage of the poverty line. Incomes above the poverty line are given a similar mirror image measure that we call 'poverty clearance'. We use a 20% poverty clearance as a guideline figure for poverty clearance over the lifetime to show a minimum level of clearance for periods of the lifetime that can potentially provide for poorer subsequent periods.

poverty clearance of 121%, rising to 125% as earnings rise parallel to the poverty line but loan repayments rise with prices alongside tax and National Insurance thresholds and his rent and Council Tax. When he finishes paying back the student loan and starts saving, this raises both his net disposable earnings (as the loan repayments were taken from earnings through PAYE) and income, but he also begins to earn income from the savings he takes out for a deposit to buy his home. The result is that his poverty clearance grows immediately to 155% and then climbs to 212% at the point when he buys his home aged 33. At that point the interest payments on the mortgage and the loss of income from savings reduce his net income after housing costs to a 131% poverty gap. This reflects the 'front-loaded' nature of mortgage repayments that, subject to specific mortgage deals that discount early payments and to interest rate changes, usually have their highest fixed costs at the historical point of purchase[6]. Subsequently, as his payments of mortgage interest decline relative to rising earnings, his net AHC income rises and by the age of 58, as his mortgage ends, he has a 226% poverty clearance. For the remaining years of his working life, poverty clearance declines very slowly as tax rises due to fiscal drag until at the point of retirement Mr Modal has a 221% poverty clearance.

Figure 2.4: Model lifetime: Mr Modal (poverty profile for lifetime with state pensions only: working 38 hours a week at average hourly pay from 21 to 65)

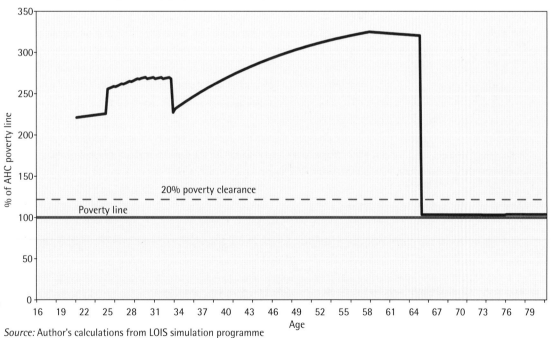

Source: Author's calculations from LOIS simulation programme

---

[6] We do not alter interest rates over the period of mortgage repayment – but if we did then the overall profile of mortgage payments would be subject to periodic variations in interest rates and thus there would be a less simple linear profile of increasing affordability over time.

Box 2.6: State pension provision

Contributory state pensions are based on the record of paid and credited NICs made over working years (16-64).

- *Basic retirement pension:* this is a flat rate pension based on a contribution record of NICs either paid while earning or credited while unemployed, at home looking after children or a disabled person, or for other limited reasons. To qualify for a full pension a person must have paid or credited contributions for nine tenths of their working life. Part-pensions are payable to those with shorter contributions periods. The pension was £77.45 per week in 2003/04.
- *State Second Pension (S2P):* this is a new secondary earnings-related pension that exists as an alternative to private pensions for those with low earnings. Those earners (not self-employed) who do not 'opt out' of state secondary provision by taking up occupational or private pensions are automatically included in the scheme. Current S2P rules are focused on the transitional entitlement of those who had contributed to SERPS (the previous version of earnings-related secondary pension). For our simulation, the rules run in a pure version of S2P. This gives rise to a pension based on earnings and is calculated according to bands of earnings: 40% of earnings of the first band, up to £11,200; 10% of earnings in the second band, from £11,200 to £25,600; and 20% of the third band of earnings above this level up to the maximum of the upper earnings limit. Cumulative totals for these earnings pools are divided by number of years of contribution from the age of 16. The earnings bands are up-rated by average earnings inflation.

Means-tested pensions
- Pension Credit: Guarantee Credit makes up income from all sources (net of tax) to a minimum income guarantee level – £102.10 per week for a single person and £155.80 per week for a couple in 2003/04 and currently available for all those aged 60 and over. The minimum entitlement age will move to 65 at some point in the future and we have used 65 for our calculations. Additional elements are paid to disabled pensioners and carers.
- Pension Credit: Savings Credit is available from the age of 65 and stops a 100% withdrawal of income above Pension Credit guarantee levels. It replaces this by supporting 60% of the difference up to a maximum total income of £140 per week for single and £204 per week for couple pensioners.

Benefits in kind for older people
An annual winter fuel allowance of £200 per annum is paid to all those aged 60 and over. Television licence fees are paid for the over seventy-fives. Prescription costs and other health-related charges are also waived for the over sixties.

Tax and NIC relief for pensions
For those who opt out of state secondary pensions, the state gives a subsidy through lower NICs and tax relief on the contributions made. This, at current standard tax rates, is 28p in the pound.

Improving pension provision

Mr Modal's significant lifetime risk of poverty is in retirement as he relies solely on state-run pension provision. **Box 2.7** discusses the main aspects of state pension rules, subsidies and provision. How can he improve his pension levels to improve his poverty profile in retirement? If we adopt a target poverty clearance of 20% for retirement, what level of pension investment and contribution could raise his poverty clearance from 4% to 20%? LOIS can re-simulate his lifetime for different forms of pension provision but simulating pension provision is very complex and involves not only contributions from the individual but also contributions from the state in tax and National Insurance relief as well as from his employer, perhaps. Our approach is to use two very different types of alternative pension provision:

- A pension run by his employer that guarantees a percentage of final earnings – a so-called 'defined benefit' scheme that we call 'occupational pension'.
- A pension run by an insurance or other financial services provider that invests contributions made into a fund, which, at the point of retirement, is used to purchase an annuity. This is called a 'defined contribution' scheme and we call it 'private pension'.

Occupational pension

There are two main forms of pensions provided by employers. They can organise and contribute to a private pension that looks very like a normal money purchase pension of a defined contributions type (sometimes called a group personal pension). The alternative is the more traditional occupational pension that provides for a pension based on final earnings – or a defined benefit scheme and often called 'superannuation'. We use this latter type as the first alternative for Mr Modal and as the primary form of occupational pension. Recent evidence suggests that this form of occupational provision is losing ground, with employers restricting new entrants to schemes and favouring more market-based alternatives in which the risk to the employer is minimised.

Mr Modal's employer runs a scheme into which he pays 6% of his earnings, a contribution that matches the most common rate of contribution to such schemes found in the Government Actuary's survey in 2000 (GAD, 2003). **Box 2.7** describes the details of defined benefit occupational pension schemes. What difference would this make to his retirement income and would this also provide a 20% poverty clearance during retirement?

The pension scheme for Mr Modal uses an accrual rate of 1/60th of final salary (with no additional tax free lump sum at the point of retirement). Mr Modal has worked and contributed for 44 years and his final earnings are projected to be 44/60ths of the average of his final year's employment and this represents a pension of approximately 64% of average earnings at the age of 65.

Figure 2.5 shows the revised lifetime income components for Mr Modal assuming he joined the occupational pension scheme. Mr Modal pays less tax and National Insurance over his working life as he is opted out of the state NI system and received tax relief on his contributions to the pension scheme. At age 65, he ceases earning and receives both the basic retirement pension alongside his occupational pension. These are both taxable income and he pays Income Tax – however, his liability to pay NICs ends at 65. Over the time of his retirement his pension income declines as both pensions only rise with price inflation and their combined relative value against average earnings falls.

Figure 2.6 shows Mr Modal's resulting lifetime poverty profile from being a member of the occupational pension scheme. The obvious difference to the previous poverty profile in **Figure 2.2** is that an occupational pension provides a very significant level of poverty clearance throughout retirement. Poverty clearance at age 65 is 181% and this very large clearance reflects only a small decrease in disposable income at the point of retirement. This comes about from the combination of several factors; the occupational pension is around 60% of earnings and is paid in addition to state pension and, simultaneously, NIC liability ends and Income Tax falls due to age allowances. After the age of 65, income declines relative to the poverty line as both state and occupational pensions are only up-rated by price inflation. Over the whole of retirement this falls to a 108% clearance at death aged 81.

Box 2.7: Defined benefit occupational pensions

The contributions into an occupational pension of this type are paid either by the employer alone or by both employer and employee. Pensions are calculated according to (Ward, 2003a, 2003b):

- Length of time in the scheme.
- The earnings used to calculate the pension 'final pensionable earnings':
    - these may be the average of your earnings in your last year's employment, or
    - an average over the last few years (most commonly three years).
- The 'accrual rate':
    - this is the ratio of earnings for every year of membership; usually these are
        - 1/80th which gives one half of final earnings over 40 years, or
        - 1/60th which gives two thirds of final earnings over 40 years.
- The choice of receiving an element of pension as a lump sum (tax free) awarded alongside a regular pension at the time of retirement – such lump sums are often attached to a lower 1/80th accrual rate for the accompanying pension.

Employers' contributions average around 8% of earnings in 2000 (GAD, 2003) but this level of contribution depends on the funding of the pension according to its actuarial liabilities. Tax and NIC relief is paid to the employee contributor.

Private pension

What if Mr Modal had to rely completely on a money purchase pension from a private pension provider? Simulating choices and opportunities is very difficult and complex. There are two main choices that face Mr Modal at different times in a money purchase scheme: first, with whom to contribute to build up a pension fund, and then second, when he retires, from whom to purchase an annuity with his fund. **Box 2.8** outlines the main features of money purchase schemes for both building a pension savings fund and the purchase of annuities.

Figure 2.5: Model lifetime: Mr Modal (income and tax profile with an occupational final salary pension)

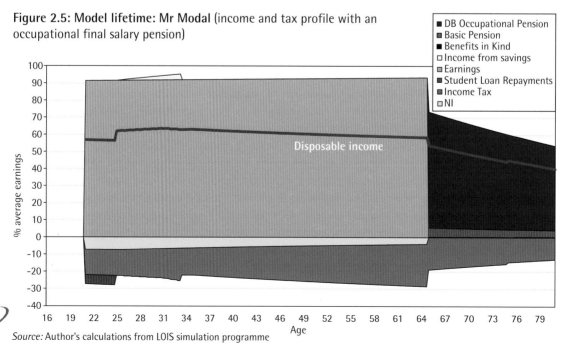

Source: Author's calculations from LOIS simulation programme

Figure 2.6: Model lifetime: Mr Modal (poverty profile with final salary occupational pension)

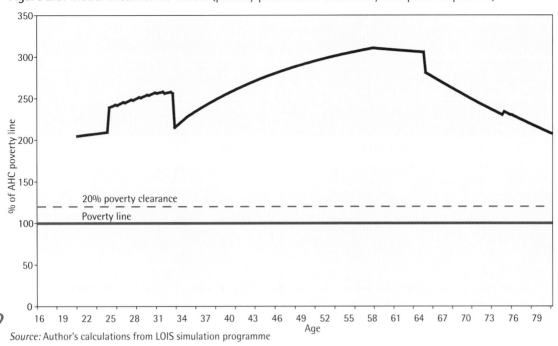

Source: Author's calculations from LOIS simulation programme

As **Box 2.8** outlines, private money purchase pension provision is characterised by choice, uncertainty (both plannable and unplannable) and information difficulties. In all of our simulations for Mr Modal we assume that this choice is made during the working life as early as possible at the point of entering the labour market at the age of 21. This optimises potential saving to the fund and pension outcomes. We also assume that, in the same way as defined benefit pensions, people will be trying to protect their living standards in relative terms. This assumption means that we can compare the outcomes from money purchase schemes to both state pension provision, in effect the poverty clearance given by Pension Credit Guarantee, and to the defined benefit occupation pension already discussed.

How much would Mr Modal have to contribute to produce a satisfactory retirement income? This question turns on how much he contributes and how well his funds and annuity purchase perform. Our approach is as follows: first, we set up a series of money purchase assumptions that can simulate the choices for both funding and annuity purchase. Fund choices are between stakeholder or non-stakeholder – with charges set at 1% for stakeholder and 2.5% for non-stakeholder. For both fund choices we employ the same assumption of a 6.5% return on investment used by the DWP in the Pensions Green Paper (DWP, 2002). Annuity choices are based on two outcomes. First, we use the LOIS annuity equation on the accumulated funds using life expectancy based on the latest Government Actuary life tables (GAD, 2004). Effectively this means a pure annuity with no commission or charges on a single life. Alternatively we show the effect of the *best performing* inflation-safeguarded annuity[7].

---

[7] See Table 2.4. We assume the same underlying proportional annuity outcomes on the actual fund as were given on a fund of £100,000.

Box 2.8: Private money purchase defined benefit pensions

The fund

The government regulates the pensions industry and has set up *stakeholder pensions* that have stipulated maximum administration charges and carry no entry and exit charges (a levy on early years of contributions to meet the transaction costs of setting up the fund and penalties for leaving or ceasing to contribute). Stakeholder pensions have a maximum administration charge of 1% annually of the total fund value; however, there is pressure to raise this to 1.5%. The argument is that such regulation has tended to make such funds have lower performance to match the increased risk to the fund holder and to have introduced a lowering of charges more widely across the board. Table 2.2 shows the differences made to Mr Modal's personal pension fund according to the charges and type of scheme entered into. We estimate these differences using 11% of Mr Modal's earnings for the whole period from his entering work at 21 to his retirement. Pension saving rates are estimated at 6.5% in accordance with government projections (DWP, 2002).

Table 2.2 shows the clear advantage of stakeholder pensions over other forms of pensions if funds accumulate at the same rate – over 44 years Mr Modal's fund is 47% higher because of reduced administration charges and no entry charge.

Table 2.2: Pension fund differences

Pension type	Entry charges (%)	Number of years	Administration charge (%)	Fund at 65
Stakeholder	na	na	1%	£1,212,721
Non-stakeholder	5	5	2.5%	£821,912

Annuity purchase

Annuity rates fluctuate over time, changing in part with the economic cycle. In 1999, rates were around 7% and at the time of writing they have fallen to between 4% and 5%. Table 2.3 shows the effect of a change in annuity rates from 4.5% to 3% on an annuity of £50,000 in today's prices for a man aged 65 with a predicted longevity of 81 (as per Mr Modal).

Table 2.3: Annuity income per week at the age of 65 from £50,000 at changing annuity rates

Annuity rate (%)	Weekly income (£)
4.5	82.78
4.0	82.78
3.5	79.77
3.0	76.81

However, there are other risks and uncertainties with annuity purchase. First, the market provider that holds your fund may not be the best value provider of an annuity from it. Second, the annuity provider will calculate the actuarial risk of long life and pay accordingly. Thus, those with shorter life expectancy – men, smokers and those with ill health, for instance – will receive higher annuities than women, non-smokers and the chronically ill. Third, until you approach providers with bona fide details of your fund, there is little opportunity to obtain information about charges and commissions in setting up the annuity, nor other underlying assumptions. Fourth, there is a wide and growing level of choice in annuity products, with combinations of inflation proofing, single and couple life products and ways of ensuring higher pay-outs if longevity is very short.

All these factors mean that choice is potentially great but is accompanied by considerable information failure because large elements of information is only knowable at the point of retirement and thus not entirely 'plannable' to any large extent. However, choice means that there is a range of annuity outcomes for the same fund. If we take the same amount of fund and look at current variation between the top five annuity providers only then Table 2.4 shows the differences that can occur in retirement income for a man at 65 taking a single life annuity.

Even between the top five providers, as chosen by *Pensions World* magazine, there is a 13% difference in pension outcomes for non-inflation guaranteed annuities and a 3% to 4% difference in inflation guaranteed annuities.

Table 2.4: Annuities compared for a 65-year-old man for a £100,000 fund

Basis of annuity	Weekly annuity
Annuities without inflation safeguard	
Best performer	£162.28
5th best performer	£141.23
Annuities with inflation safeguard (3%)	
Best performer	£106.95
5th best performer	£103.38

Source: *Pensions World* pensions statistics, March 2004

LOIS' annuity model

Underlying an annuity is the calculation made on what income will come from an investment over a set period of time (the expected remaining years of life). This can be expressed as an equation as follows:

$$Annuity = annuity\ rate \times fund \div [1-(1+r)^{-t}]$$

Where *t* is equal to the number of years of life expectancy. We currently use an annuity rate set at same rate for long-term gilts at 4.5% (*Financial Times*, March 2004).

The combination of choices of fund and annuity thus gives *four* alternative private money purchase pensions:

- *Pension A (benchmark):* stakeholder with LOIS equation with contributions sufficient to give a 20% poverty clearance in retirement.
- *Pension B:* stakeholder with the best inflation-proofed performer on the same contribution level.
- *Pension C:* non-stakeholder with LOIS equation on the same contribution level.
- *Pension D:* non-stakeholder with the best inflation-proofed provider on the same contribution level.

In shorthand, Pension A will give 'best value' because charges and commissions are set to a minimum, while Pension D will give 'worst value' because charges and commissions are the largest of the four. We remind readers that we are not showing the pension providers at their worst value – because even Pension D is based on the 'best' current provider, not the worst. Additionally, we must also point out that losses from charges and commissions may be made up by higher returns in a more 'hands on' administered fund.

What contributions will Mr Modal have to make? For the sake of comparison we use the same contribution level that was used for Mr Modal's occupational pension, 6% of earnings. Other money purchase choices, Pensions B, C and D, are then simulated to show their outcomes for the same 6% of earnings contribution. This allows us to directly compare pension outcomes from the same contribution rate both between defined benefit and our four money purchase choices and to the basic state provision.

Figure 2.7 shows the four private pension outcomes expressed as a percentage of average earnings from age 65 onwards, all based on a contribution of 6% of earnings. Pension A, invested in a stakeholder fund and then purchasing a full annuity without charges or commission, gives rise to an income that qualifies for no further assistance from means-

Figure 2.7: Model lifetime: Mr Modal (income components aged 65 and over for four private defined contribution pensions: income as a % of average earnings)

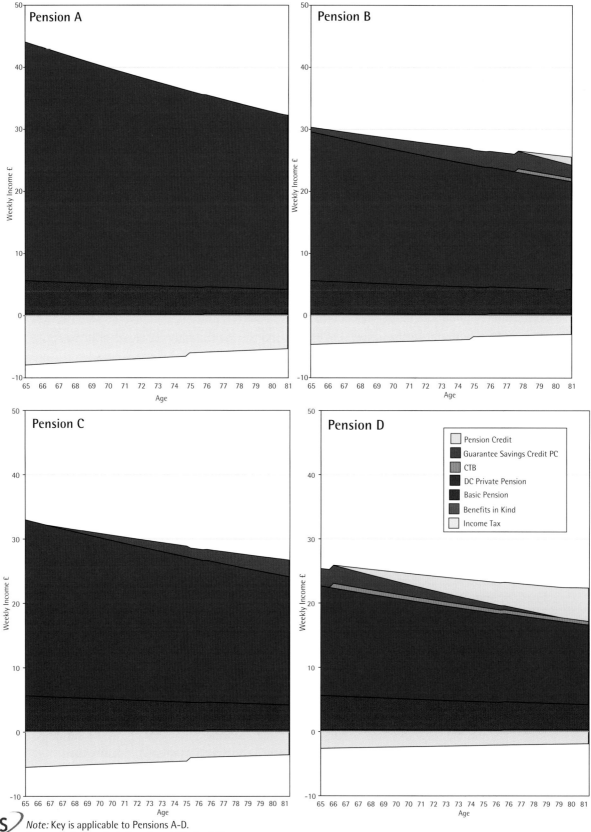

tested benefits. At 65 the pension is worth 38% of average earnings and then declines over time as its price indexation falls relative to earnings. Pension B, invested in a stakeholder fund and then purchasing an annuity based on the best current provider of price-indexed annuities gives rise to a much lower pension, 24% of average earnings at the age of 65, which gives rise to an entitlement to Savings Credit pension credits immediately and then, as the pension continues to decline over time relative to Pension Credit levels, it declines to a point at age 78 when Pension Credit is paid and Council Tax Benefit alongside it. Pension C, invested in a non-stakeholder fund and then purchasing a full annuity without charges or commission, gives rise to a pension that is 27% of average earnings at 65 and that becomes supplemented by Savings Credit pension credits within three years. Last, Pension D, invested in a non-stakeholder fund and purchasing an annuity based on the best current provider of price-indexed annuities only gives rise to a pension of 17% of average earnings and that within one year falls into Pension Credit Guarantee levels.

It is worth reminding readers that the inputs are identical to all four pension outcomes – both from Mr Modal and his payments and from government in the form of tax relief and NI rebates. However, they lead to very different outcomes – both in terms of income and poverty coverage for Mr Modal and also subsequent spending and tax income for the government[8].

Figure 2.8 shows the poverty profiles of all the pension options discussed so far for Mr Modal, from relying only on state pensions, to the best option of an occupational defined benefit scheme and then the four simulated options for private pensions.

Figure 2.8 highlights two main features of individual-based strategies of shifting income over the life cycle: first, that investment in pensions or other saving behaviour lowers current income at the point of saving. This is where the concept of poverty clearance becomes very important in lifetime profiles. To shift money to prevent poverty at one part of the lifetime should not mean that the result is poverty over the period from which it has been

Figure 2.8: Model lifetime: Mr Modal (lifetime poverty profiles for all simulated pension options: State pensions only and five outcomes from 6% contributions to non-state pension)

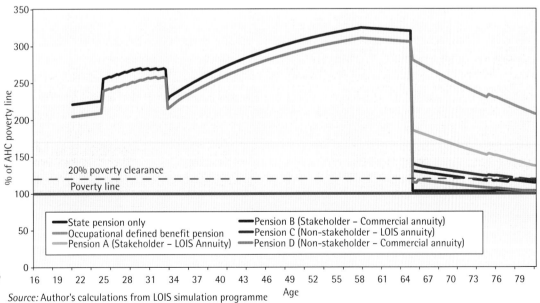

Source: Author's calculations from LOIS simulation programme

---

shifted. In simple terms, is it sensible to go into poverty now by saving to avoid poverty in the future? When thinking about lifetime income and poverty profiles we therefore bring in a poverty clearance level of 20% – both to reflect a margin of living standards that avoids poverty over the lifetime and to provide a cushion of income above Pension Credit Guarantee levels in retirement. In Mr Modal's case, contributions to pension saving lower his relative living standards during his working life but these do reduce income close to a 20% poverty clearance level.

Second, that the *outcomes* of such pension investment and savings behaviour are very varied in their potential to protect such levels of poverty clearance in retirement. Pension A – the best value approach of stakeholder funds and no commission annuity – gives an 85% poverty clearance at retirement (a lot less than the defined benefit occupational scheme, where the employer has also contributed) and a 37% poverty clearance at point of death. None of the other money purchase choices protect retirement income against a 20% poverty clearance threshold. Pension C (non-stakeholder and LOIS annuity) gives a 40% poverty clearance level at 65 but falls to 18% at 81. Pension B (non-stakeholder and LOIS annuity) gives a 30% poverty clearance at retirement falling to 14% and last, Pension D provides only a 15% poverty clearance that falls to below Pension Credit Guarantee levels.

Gender and the average lifetime: Ms Modal

Not all 'average' people are men, and while the modal employee may be male, women represent 55% of the workforce[9] and face discrimination and different forms of gender penalties in pay and conditions of work. What difference does being female have on the average case? To assess this question in the first instance, we maintain all the assumptions of Mr Modal, life expectancy, tenure, higher education, retirement age, and so on, but alter two factors:

- We reduce earnings by the average 'gender penalty' on pay. This means that we keep hours of work constant at 38 but reduce the average hourly wage to that of women: £10.56 per hour.
- We calculate pensions on the basis of average female life expectancy. To be consistent with Mr Modal and to allow direct comparison we simulate the same age of death at 81.

We call this simulated lifetime Ms Modal – and she can be thought of as the twin sister of Mr Modal with a parallel life course. However, it is not quite possible to have an exactly parallel life course because the pay penalty has repercussions on Ms Modal's ability to pay off her student loan and subsequently save the deposit to purchase her home. Having lower pay than her twin brother means that both these take longer and she eventually purchases her home at age 34¾. But the main question we ask in Ms Modal's model lifetime is how the gender penalty on earnings affects her pension choices. **Figure 2.9** shows the lifetime poverty profiles to explore three simulated pension choices that are consistent with each other and consistent with our previous discussion of Mr Modal. The first pension 'choice' is that she works alongside her brother for the employer who runs the same occupational pension scheme that pays a defined benefit final salary scheme based on a 1/60 accrual rate. This gives her a pension of 42% of average earnings and a poverty clearance at retirement of 142% that falls to 80% when she dies (for the sake of consistent comparison and argument) on the same day as her twin. Her other pension choices are based on money purchase defined contribution pensions that would obtain a 20% poverty clearance throughout

---

[9] In 2003 (spring quarter) 14.88 million women aged 16-59 out of a total of 27.16 million in employment, including men aged 16-64 (*Labour Market Trends*, Table A1, April 2004).

Figure 2.9: Model lifetime: Ms Modal (lifetime poverty profiles for all three simulated money pension options: to obtain 20% poverty clearance throughout retirement)

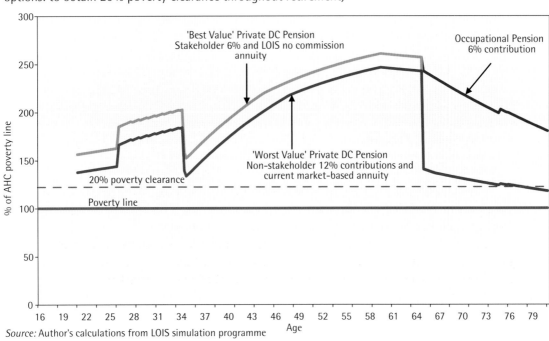

Source: Author's calculations from LOIS simulation programme

retirement. This again means that the LOIS simulations work backwards from this target pension outcome to the annuity sum needed to obtain it and then to the contribution rate needed to get to that sum.

Figure 2.9 shows the outcome of what we can crudely call the best value and worst value choices – previously discussed as Pension options A and D for Mr Modal. The best value private pension builds its fund in a stakeholder account and then has a commission-free annuity. This enables Ms Modal to contribute 6% of her earnings to receive a pension that gives her a 40% poverty clearance at retirement and 20% at death. The worst value option builds funds in a non-stakeholder fund and has a current leading market annuity outcome. While this gives her the same pension outcome, she has to double her contributions – 12% of her earnings because of charges and commission in both the fund and annuity purchase. The effect of this higher level of contribution is to make the whole of Ms Modal's working lifetime considerably poorer in relative terms, and at the worst point of her working life – the point of purchasing her home and paying the highest ratio of mortgage interest to earnings – she dips towards poverty and only has a 35% poverty clearance. This dip in poverty clearance is mostly due to the combination of house purchase and a lower earnings level compared to Mr Modal.

The average single lifetime: conclusions and summary

Mr and Ms Modal's lifetime profiles give them average earnings with no children or interruptions from work. They receive no help from benefits or tax credits during their working lives. They pay tax and NI and their return for this in lifetime taxes and benefits is a very low rate of basic pension (around 5% of earnings when they retire) and a top-up pension – S2P – that does not take them above the social minimum income for pensioners and gives them an income of around 4% above the poverty line when they retire. Their biggest lifetime risk is thus the threat of having incomes at the margins of poverty in their retirement.

Responding to this risk means saving for retirement, thus smoothing income over their lifetimes by putting money aside while they are working in order to have higher living standards in retirement. The opportunities to do so and the choices available, however, are not open ended but structurally constrained.

The most secure option in terms of pension levels is to join a defined benefit scheme – usually as an employer-run occupational pension. However, access to such schemes is declining as more employers try to limit their financial risks and commitments to occupational pensions. The National Association of Pension Funds found that in their 2003 survey "for the last three years there has been significant growth in the percentage of private sector final salary schemes closed to new members.... Nearly three quarters (72%) of respondents who had closed a final salary scheme said their main reason for doing so was cost containment" (NAPF, 2003, p 2). Public sector occupational schemes are, in general, more secure but overall the move from employers out from defined benefit schemes to defined contribution schemes (with a resulting lower contemporary contribution costs on their part and lower long-term risks) is seen as a crisis across the Trades Union movement.

The alternative – saving with a private pension provider for a defined contribution money purchase scheme (whether helped by the employer or not) – is more risky for the individual. We have shown that outcomes are more uncertain and costs of contribution are higher to individuals than occupational pensions – even to achieve a desired modest level of poverty clearance in old age. Additionally, while the regulation of commission and charges in stakeholder pensions assists in ensuring better value outcomes, the issue of charges and commission can still radically affect pension outcomes and for many is an additional and unknowable future risk when they draw their annuities.

The Modals have levels of income that enable them to invest more to protect their living standards in retirement but will face the full force of market risk in doing so unless they can join a defined benefit occupational scheme. While 'simplicity, security and choice' are excellent aims for policy (DWP, 2002), there appear to be structural impediments to optimal combinations of and trade-offs between these aims. These impediments will be greater for those on lower earnings levels than the Modals, and it is to these model lifetimes that we now turn.

Low-paid lifetimes

… it takes all the running you can do to keep in the same place.

If you want to get somewhere else you must run twice as fast. (Lewis Caroll, *Through the looking glass*)

This chapter examines the policy packages available for the low paid and the lifetime policy implications of low pay. We address two main questions:

- What are the lifetime opportunities and risk of poverty for those with low pay and how do these compare to the 'average lifetime'?
- How much would low pay have to rise, and when, to make opportunities more equal with Mr Modal and reduce the risks of lifetime poverty?

In order to compare a low-paid lifetime to our average case we maintain the approach of using a lifetime un-partnered single man. We call this model lifetime Mr Meager.

Low-paid lifetime

While it would be perfect to make all of Mr Meager's lifetime details resemble Mr Modal's for comparative reasons, it makes little sense in reality to do so. Mr Meager's earnings are low in part because he is less skilled and educated than average. This means that to simulate a lifetime on low pay Mr Meager should not be a graduate. We simulate Mr Meager as leaving school at the age of 16 and going straight into work, which means that he has a longer working life but the extra years will not make up total lifetime earnings to the same level. A low-paid working lifetime also restricts access to owner-occupation and constrains other lifetime investment decisions such as private pensions. To make Mr Meager more comparable with Mr Modal, we simulate him living with his mother until he is 21, thus replicating Mr Modal's entry into rented housing at that age after he had finished higher education.

Mr Meager's rent is the same as Mr Modal's prior to him buying a house: a weekly rent of £86.50 and a Council Tax of £10.70 per week. These housing and Council Tax costs are based on renting in the private sector (without special needs or circumstances it is unlikely that Mr Meager would gain access to the social rented sector), and both rents and Council Tax will rise with prices over the lifetime as our principal assumption. **Box 3.1** gives more detail about the rented housing sector and rent levels.

Box 3.1: Rents and renting

The rented sector is made up of a social sector and a private sector that differ in both rent levels and rent inflation profiles.

The *social sector* is made up of both local authorities and other Registered Social Landlords (RSLs) such as housing associations.

- RSL average rents in 2002 were £55.81 per week and since 1997 have risen by an average of 3.6% per year.
- Local authority average rents in 2002 were £51.39 per week and since 1997 have risen by an average of 3.7% per year.

Due to overall compositional changes and the move away from local authority to RSL housing over the period, overall average rent inflation for the whole social sector since 1997 was 3.9%.

The *private sector* is made up of a stock that is subject to different historic rules for rent regulation. There is an older stock of lettings with registered rents and more recent lettings under different rules. Overall average rents in 2002/03 were £274 per week and have risen by an average of 7% per year since 1997.

Guidance rents for simulation

The rents paid by low-income families are not the average for many reasons – time of letting, size, location, and so on. We adopt the price conventions used by the DWP in their Tax Benefit Model

Table 3.1: Guidance rents for model lifetimes with low pay (£ per week) (2003-04)

	Local authority	Private
No children	43.76	86.50
One child	47.52	94.30
Two or more children	52.92	132.20

Tables (2003a) when simulating rents for this report. This convention uses rent levels based on family composition and sector and is shown in Table 3.1.

Low pay can be defined in a number of ways. We adopt a measure based on 60% of median hourly pay (New Earnings Survey, 2003). Mr Meager works for £5.88 an hour but otherwise his hours of work and earnings inflation figures are the same as Mr Modal's (38 hours a week and 4.55% per annum).

Figure 3.1 shows the lifetime income profile for Mr Meager. He pays tax and National Insurance during his working life but, like Mr Modal, receives no benefits or tax credits to help him, despite his low pay. In this first simulation of his model lifetime he does not opt out of state pensions but his annual income of around £11,620 in today's prices means that he is the bottom portion of the income band of potential pension savers – those who are not currently saving but who are not on a low income (DWP, 2002) and also in the lower bands of those identified as potential stakeholder pension customers with annual incomes in 1998 prices of between £9,000 to £20,000[10] (DWP, 1998). In this model lifetime, his retirement income is composed of basic state pension, S2P and Pension Credit Basic Guarantee along with Housing Benefits and Council Tax Benefits to pay these liabilities. **Box 3.2** describes the Housing and Council Tax Benefit programmes.

---

[10] An annual income of £9,000 in 1998 at the DWP's assumptions of average earnings growth of 4.55% comes to £11,242 over six years to 2004.

Box 3.2: Housing and Council Tax Benefits

Benefits to assist with rent and Council Tax pay 100% of eligible liability both for those who claim the safety net social assistance benefit Income Support and its sister benefit for the unemployed, income-based Jobseeker's Allowance, which is paid at exactly the same rates. 100% payment of both benefits is also ensured for those who receive Pension Credit (Guarantee Credit) – the equivalent but more generous means-tested safety net for those aged 65 (currently 60) and over.

For those with incomes above Income Support and Pension Credit levels, then the amount of help with rent and Council Tax is reduced on a taper. For every £1 that net income (after tax and National Insurance) is above Income Support or Pension Credit levels, entitlement to Housing Benefit and Council Tax Benefit is reduced as follows:

- 65% for Housing Benefit for rent
- 20% for Council Tax Benefit.

There are deductions made from the rent eligible for Housing Benefit if someone lives in your home and is expected to assist with paying the rent – non-dependant deductions. LOIS does not calculate these as only partners and children (dependants) are included in calculations. However, we use the amounts for non-dependant deductions when estimating housings costs for Mr Meager and others when they are living in the parental home.

See CPAG (2003) and Tolleys (2003) for more details.

There is, however, a mystery with Mr Meager – he is low paid and is paying a substantial rent that represents around 39% of his gross earnings and 46% of his take home pay on his rent. Why doesn't he qualify for the benefits that could support him during his working life – and potentially assist him to save towards a better pension? To address this question, we re-simulate his lifetime using *current prices* – that is, assuming no earnings or price inflation, and when we do so we estimate that Mr Meager would receive help with just under £6 per week Housing Benefit towards his rent. However, even in current prices Mr Meager would never qualify for Working Tax Credit as eligibility tapers out at earnings below 60%

Figure 3.1: Model lifetime: Mr Meager (lifetime income and tax profile 38 hours at 60% of median hourly wage)

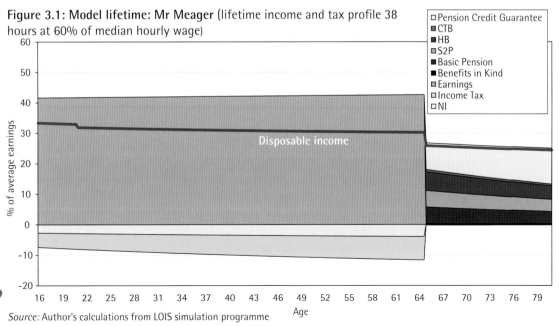

Source: Author's calculations from LOIS simulation programme

Box 3.3: Working Tax Credit and in-work benefits package

Introduced in April 2003, Working Tax Credit is payable to all employees whose earnings fall into the threshold for assistance if they:

- have children and work 16 hours or more;
- are aged 25 and over and work 30 hours or more.

Working Tax Credit calculation is made up of a number of different elements:

- basic element
- disability element
- lone parent/couple element
- 30-hour week element
- severe disability element
- 50+ element (for one year on return to work)
- childcare element.

Entitlement is made up of the appropriate qualifying elements that make up 'maximum Working Tax Credit' and then income is compared to the income threshold figure (£5,060 in 2003/04) and maximum Working Tax Credit is reduced by 37% of every pound in excess of the threshold.

See CPAG (2003) and Tolleys (2003) for more details.

Figure 3.2: In-work benefits, Income Support and poverty for single low-waged person aged 25 or more (current prices 2003/04, 16-40 hours per week)

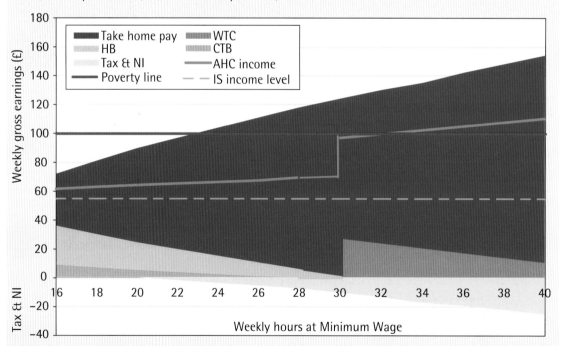

Source: Author's calculations and DWP (2003b) programme

In-work benefits and low pay: households with no children

LOIS lifetime simulations in this report all use up-rated and inflated calculations over the lifetime and this means that today's entitlement profile can be lost through projection into the medium to long term. Figure 3.2 therefore shows entitlement to Housing Benefit, Council Tax Benefit and Working Tax Credit based on 2003/04 prices on a hypothetical individual who can work between 16 and 40 hours a week for the National Minimum Wage using the same levels of rent and Council Tax as outlined previously, and shows entitlement to in-work benefits and liabilities for tax and National Insurance based on DWP Tax Benefit Tables (DWP, 2003a). Figure 3.2 shows that Housing Benefit and Council Tax Benefit help an individual on National Minimum Wage levels but do not prevent poverty up to 30 hours a week. At that point Working Tax Credit is paid, no Housing Benefit or Council Tax Credit is payable but this brings the individual roughly up to the poverty line. AHC income profiles are at a small gradient either side of 30 hours due to the combination of tax and National Insurance liability and withdrawal of means-tested benefits as income rises (see the discussion of marginal tax rates in Chapter 4). When this profile is repeated for a younger worker aged less than 25 then Housing Benefit and Council Tax Benefit never lift them above the poverty line – even at 40 hours. Figure 3.3 shows the resulting profile.

Figure 3.3: In-work benefits, Income Support and poverty for single low-waged person aged under 25 (current prices 2003/04, 16-40 hours per week)

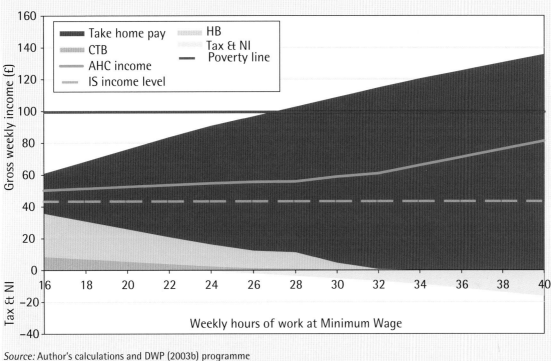

Source: Author's calculations and DWP (2003b) programme

of the median[11]. **Box 3.3** outlines the basic rules for Working Tax Credit and explains how entitlement to Working Tax Credit alongside Housing Benefit and Council Tax Benefit would apply in contemporary cross-sectional circumstances based on current prices.

The Low Pay Commission has suggested that the National Minimum Wage should rise slightly above average earnings in the short to medium term to have an impact (LPC, 2003). This means that low pay at levels above the National Minimum Wage will also rise at or around average earnings inflation and that assistance from means-tested benefits like Working Tax Credit, Housing Benefit and Council Tax Benefit will erode over time as

---

[11] Even at National Minimum Wage levels, LOIS estimated very little entitlement to Working Tax Credit over a low-paid lifetime. However, this is most true for those who only qualify when they reach 25 (that is, those with no children) because each model lifetime starts at 16 and inflation and up-rating over nine years prior to 25 have reduced entitlement to Working Tax Credit above and beyond what would be expected if a lifetime was begun at a later age. This means that, on income levels alone, individuals on the National Minimum Wage would qualify prior to their 25th birthday but are excluded from eligibility on age grounds.

Figure 3.4: Inflation, Minimum Wage and means-tested in-work benefit entitlement thresholds over the next 50 years (real growth in 2003/04 prices)

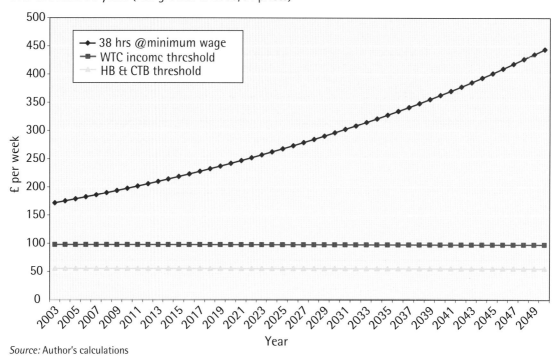

Source: Author's calculations

even low-paid earnings will rise faster than the income thresholds for entitlement to these benefits. This is shown in **Figure 3.4** above.

The fact that rising earnings lift people out of entitlement to Working Tax Credit and other in-work benefits is no bad thing in itself as they have higher standards of living. But **Figure 3.5** shows the lifetime poverty profile for Mr Meager and shows that this erosion of entitlement is not accompanied by lower poverty risk. Indeed, we know from our discussion in **Box 3.3** that the current configuration of tax credits and in-work benefits would *today* lift Mr Meager to around the poverty line once he was aged above 25. However, once the system is allowed to up-rate and inflation is allowed to occur, both of which are simulated in line with current government's assumptions, Mr Meager is actually below poverty levels in his early twenties as he does not qualify for Working Tax Credit and pays rent and then subsequently spends his whole life in and around the margins of poverty. Entering the private rented housing market at 21 puts Mr Meager below poverty, having previously had a poverty clearance of 40% while living with his parents. After the age of 21 his income rises in relative terms as the rent he is paying is rising with prices behind the growth in Mr Meager's earnings until at the age of 64 he obtains a 26% poverty clearance. At 65 he falls into Pension Credit Guarantee and retires on a consistent poverty clearance of 4% – replicating the first results from Mr Modal when there was a reliance on state pensions.

The high likelihood of low-waged youth poverty is something that will affect lifetime outcomes. First, it will have knock-on lifetime implications for parents if the young people are living in the parental home – potentially affecting parental ability to save for retirement, for instance. However, it is also important for the individual lifetime because of increased reliance on individual lifetime earnings to fund pensions. Holding everything else constant, Mr Meager would have to save more and for longer than Mr Modal to achieve a level of poverty clearance in his retirement because his earnings are lower. Therefore, not protecting living standards for young people will have cumulative impacts on later life and will delay the ability to save for retirement. While it is obvious that the sooner people save for retirement the better and easier it is, it has to be equally recognised that constraints on retirement are not constant over the lifetime but higher in youth – and especially so if low paid.

Figure 3.5: Model lifetime: Mr Meager (lifetime poverty profile 38 hours at 60% of median hourly wage)

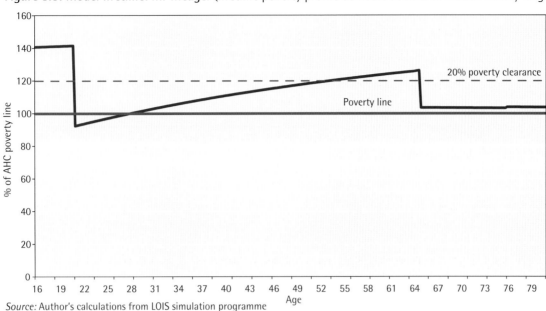

Source: Author's calculations from LOIS simulation programme

Tenure, inequality and lifetime poverty

Besides a higher likelihood of poverty caused by lower earnings, Mr Meager's lifetime risks of poverty differ from Mr Modal's through tenure; he rents while Mr Modal buys his home. This raises two structural questions about lifetime poverty profiles: first, how does renting potentially affect poverty incidence and, second, how does the difference between renting and owner-occupation affect the differences in lifetime poverty profiles?

What effect do rent levels and rent inflation have on lifetime poverty? We have already seen that changes in housing costs (rent) can affect Mr Meager's poverty profile. **Figure 3.5** showed the large step-change deterioration in poverty profile at the point at which Mr Meager leaves the parental home and starts to rent independently. This one-off change in costs together with the overall trends in small margins of poverty clearance (around the 20% poverty clearance objective that we previously employed to assess Mr Modal's lifetime) mean that the issue of rent level may potentially seriously affect opportunities and living standards over Mr Meager's lifetime and especially so when we are using an AHC income poverty measure. **Figure 3.6** shows the effect of four different rent and rent inflation assumptions on lifetime poverty. Our baseline assumption has previously been shown above in **Figure 3.5** and is shown again as the **dark blue** line, and this represents living in a private rent at the standard rents used for simulation that rise with prices. The **mauve** line shows the same rent but rising at the current rate of rent increases since 1997, 6.8%. The effect of this assumption is dramatic; with rent rising faster than earnings, Mr Meager's poverty gap grows, over time. He receives Housing Benefit and thus there is a small step-change improvement at age 25 when he falls into higher entitlement thresholds, but otherwise this choice is basically unsustainable in both market and life chances outcomes. No rental market could sustain such price increases for poorer tenants and there would be some point at which there would be price stabilisation, hopefully. But in poverty terms, the growing poverty gap reaches 34% at the age of 64.

On the other hand, a low rent helps poverty clearance and the light blue line shows the effect of using a social rent assumption that rises with prices and that gives a steadily increasing poverty clearance over the working life until it reaches a 42% poverty clearance at

Figure 3.6: Model lifetime: Mr Meager (lifetime poverty profile: the effect of four rent level and inflation assumptions)

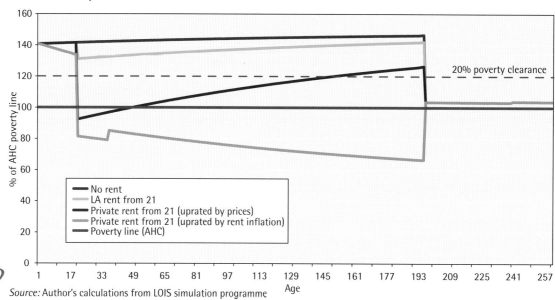

Source: Author's calculations from LOIS simulation programme

age 64. However, living in someone else's household – paying just a contribution towards the rent (calculated by using Housing Benefit non-dependant deductions), and shown by the green line in **Figure 3.6**, gives the highest poverty clearance, rising to a 46% poverty clearance at age 64.

These lifetime poverty profiles differ quite remarkably from those associated with Mr Modal's mortgage payments. Mortgage interest is based on a fixed loan amount at the beginning of the loan and thus it remains the same in nominal terms (subject to no changes in interest rates) and declines relative to earnings much faster than rent on any inflation assumption. This leads to a second question about the effect of tenure and rents on lifetime inequality between Mr Meager and Mr Modal.

Throughout this report we measure incomes in AHC terms – taking into account the liabilities for rent and mortgage interest. However, if we compare Mr Meager's and Mr Modal's income in *both* BHC and AHC terms[12] we can thus see how the effect of changing housing costs over the lifetime make their impact. **Figure 3.7** shows the *differences* between Mr Meager's and Mr Modal's income over the lifetime in both AHC and BHC terms. This comparison helps to see the effect of housing on overall income differentials over the lifetime because we are holding all other things constant – differences in earnings are constant as are retirement and other events. Indeed, to ensure complete consistency on all life profiles, we simulate both Mr Modal and Mr Meager solely relying on state pensions. **Figure 3.7** thus shows the *difference in differences* in income that can be seen in the shaded areas between the two lines. When income differences between AHC and BHC are parallel, then there is no underlying difference attributable to tenure (more exactly, attributable to housing costs that arise from tenure), but when the gap between the income lines diverges or converges then there are differences in income that relate to tenure.

Overall, **Figure 3.7** confirms that Mr Meager's income (in both AHC and BHC terms) is less than Mr Modal's – apart from in retirement – a point we discuss below. From the age of 21 (our consistent starting point) Mr Meager's and Mr Modal's differences in income are parallel

---

[12] See Box 2.5 for a discussion of the definitions of AHC and BHC income.

Figure 3.7: Lifetime income differences between Mr Meager and Mr Modal before and after housing costs

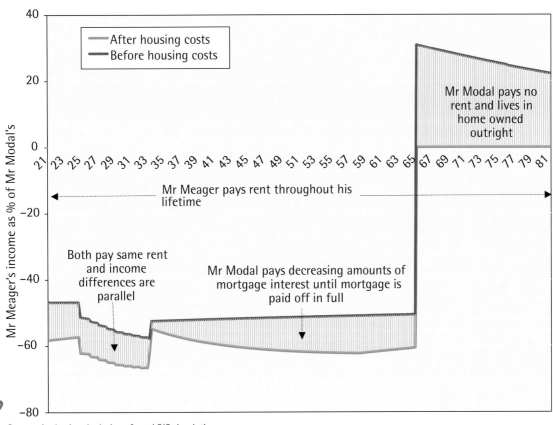

Source: Author's calculations from LOIS simulation programme

until Mr Modal buys his home at the age of 33. AHC incomes converge to a 3% difference only because that is the point at which Mr Modal purchases his home and his mortgage interest payments are highest. However, from this point onwards AHC incomes diverge and differences in differences grow as Mr Meager's AHC income falls further behind Mr Meager's as his rent rises with price inflation but Mr Modal's mortgage interest remains constant in nominal value. After the age of 59, AHC income differences stop diverging, as Mr Modal no longer pays mortgage interest and thus has no housing costs (ignoring maintenance and building insurance costs for the sake of the argument). Then at the age of 65, when both Mr Meager and Mr Modal have exactly the same income from state benefits, new differences emerge as Mr Meager's BHC income becomes 30% higher than Mr Modal's purely because he receives Housing Benefit to help him pay the rent while Mr Modal, living in his home that is owned outright, does not. This income difference seems counter-intuitive and to be the reverse of common sense.

How can a person who rents their home be better off than a person with exactly the same circumstances who owns it outright? Part of the answer lies in the fact that our income measure contains no 'implied income' from Mr Modal renting the house from himself, which in economic thinking may equalise their position but does not reflect actual incomes. A further part of the answer also reflects the fact that we have not implied maintenance and insurance costs for Mr Modal – but again these would not be at a level similar to Mr Meager's rent. This leaves us with the main reason for this anomalous and contradictory result – BHC income is a misleading measure of resources if it takes into account Housing Benefit but does not discount rent.

There are two important interim conclusions from this discussion and analysis of tenure differences: first, that tenure difference affects inequality in incomes over the lifetime and, second, that these tenure-based inequalities over the lifetime are captured best by using AHC definitions. Indeed, while these show up most clearly in a lifetime perspective, it should also be remembered that all cross-sectional income data is made up of the population being at different points in their lifetimes and is an additional reason why we prefer AHC definitions for poverty measurement.

Raising earnings capacity

Returning to Mr Meager's model lifetime, it shows a poor working life and a poor retirement. How far would Mr Meager's earnings have to rise in order to close the lifetime income differences with Mr Modal and his associated opportunities? There are two main ways in which we can think about raising Mr Meager's income to build ladders out of poverty during the lifetime:

- *A step-change increase to income:* this could reflect a single dramatic change of job or promotion but it would be highly unusual for such a one-off change to bring Mr Meager's income up to the average without some other fundamental change to his earnings capacity through training or qualification.
- *Incremental earnings progression:* earnings increase through promotion and moving jobs so that low pay is just a temporary life-cycle phenomenon. What incremental changes, and how often, would be needed to bring Mr Meager up to Mr Modal's earnings?

Making a step-change

A step-change in earnings associated with re-qualification could possibly come about by full-time higher education study or through part-time higher education or vocational qualification. **Figure 3.8** illustrates the different income outcomes from the choice of leaving work and attending a full-time higher education course and the alternative of remaining in work and qualifying to a similar level. A full-time course at a higher education institution will give rise to an earnings gap[13] followed by a period during which earnings are reduced by repayments of student loans. At present our simulations show the average student debt based on a figure of £7,400 (in current prices)[14], but proposals are in hand to raise higher education fees and thus subsequent loan amounts and repayment times. We make no attempt to simulate such changes, which at the time of writing are before Parliament, but illustrate their potential income effect in **Figure 3.8**. In the alternative, the advantage of doing a course part time or through evening courses is that current income from earnings is maintained at a higher level and any loan repayment is lower as course fees can be paid in part from current income. However, part-time qualification will take longer and the step-change in income will thus be pushed back and occur later in the working life and thus make less improvement on overall lifetime income and life chances.

We choose to illustrate the effect of a step-change based on full-time higher education that entails an earnings gap of three years and that brings low pay up to average pay on return to the labour market. Once Mr Meager has returned to work and is earning at average levels he is thus able to take up lifetime opportunities that were previously only Mr Modal's. Our

---

[13] We do not attempt to estimate income during full-time higher education study; see the previous discussion in Chapter 2.

[14] See the previous discussion in Chapter 2.

Figure 3.8: Making a step-change improvement to earnings capacity (working age [16-65] only)

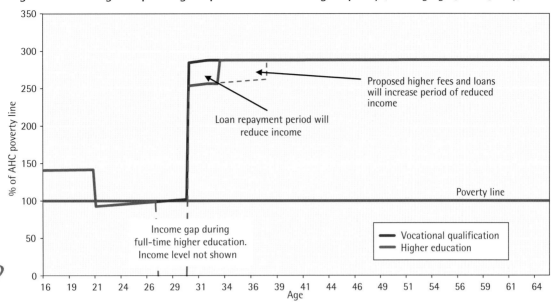

discussion so far has looked at both pensions and owner-occupation in this respect and in the limitations of this report we will focus on pensions in the first instance and then discuss how far these will interact with home ownership without full re-simulations of lifetimes that take on both. How far would such a step-change in earnings through pre-qualification improve Mr Meager's retirement income when he is presented with the same pension choices and constraints that we outlined for Mr Modal?

Our argument proceeds as follows; we base our step-change in earning capacity as completed at the age of 30 in the first instance. We then take each set of pension choices in turn, first occupational defined benefit scheme, second the 'best value' defined contribution option (Pension A from Chapter 2) and last, what may be termed the 'lowest value' defined contribution option (Pension D from Chapter 2). This gives a range of outcomes from pension choices. For each option we then re-simulate the step-change at five-yearly intervals until improvements in overall lifetime poverty profile become marginal. This enables us to explore how late a step-change can be made in the working lifetime to continue to have an impact on life chances and lifetime profiles.

Figure 3.9 shows the result of step-change re-qualification at 30, 35 and 40, combined with an occupational defined benefit pension (1/60 scheme on final year's earnings). The main driver of different outcomes from defined benefit schemes is the number of years of membership – as final salary is constant across all three simulations. A step-change at 30 provides the longest membership and gives rise to a pension with a 110% poverty clearance at retirement, falling to 57% at death. Moving the step-change forward five years to 35 reduces the pension outcome at retirement to 87%, falling to 40% at death, while moving the step-change forward a further five years to 40 produces pension outcomes to a 62% poverty clearance at retirement, falling to 20% at death, our previous minimum objective for Mr Modal's pension outcomes. This shows that promoting lifetime opportunities for low-paid people has lifetime timing constraints – the later it is left the more difficult it is to equalise lifetime outcomes and opportunities. It does not show that re-qualifying after 40 is necessarily too late, but it does suggest that Mr Meager would have to increase his pension contributions to increase his outcomes. He has a sufficiently high level of poverty clearance during his working life after re-qualification to enable him to do this, either through Additional Voluntary Contributions (AVCs) to his occupational pension or through taking out a separate additional private pension. Alternatively, he could delay retirement.

Figure 3.9: Model lifetime: Mr Meager (lifetime poverty profiles: the effect of step-change requalification at 30, 35 and 40 [outcomes for a defined benefit occupational pension (1/60) at 6% earnings contribution])

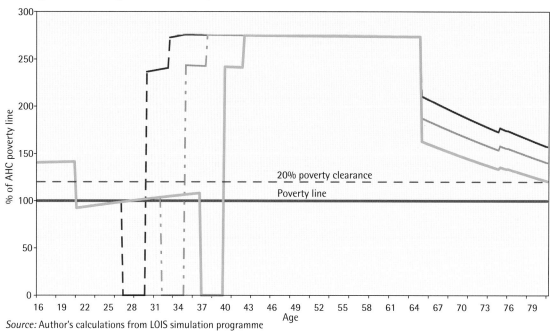

Source: Author's calculations from LOIS simulation programme

Figure 3.10 repeats these re-simulations for the so-called 'best value' defined contribution pension from the age of 30 and at subsequent five-yearly intervals. We keep the desired pension outcome constant, a 20% poverty clearance throughout retirement, in accord with our previous analysis in Chapter 2. Again, the later the step-change occurs the more difficult it is to achieve a pension outcome, but in this case there is no employer to share the costs of contribution and thus late entry leads to a greater level of contributions needed to produce a requisite pension. At 30 such contribution rates would be 8%, at 35 they would rise to 9.5%, at 40 to 11.7%, at 45 to 15% and then at 50 to 20.2%. The 20% contribution level at 50 is still below the maximum allowable for tax relief (25%) at the age of 50, and these thresholds rise with age to a maximum of 40% of earnings for those aged 61 and over. Even at the level of 20% of earnings contributions, poverty clearance during working age is 130% and this means that, while the outcome pensions are much lower (a 65% poverty clearance at 65) than that obtained though lower contributions into the defined benefit pension, there is still the opportunity to raise earnings and improve pension outcomes. However, the pension outcomes simulated in **Figure 3.10** are not those currently available on the market, and **Figure 3.11** gives a different version of events based on non-stakeholder funds and a market-based annuity.

Figure 3.11 shows much higher contribution rates required for the same outcomes because more is paid in administration charges and commission (a 2.5% annual charge on the fund and current unspecified charges and commissions on the annuity purchase). Of course, as before in Chapter 2, we are not assuming any greater return on investments for a more expensively administered fund. The step-change at 30 with this form of defined contribution requires 17% of earnings as contribution – the maximum allowed for tax relief at this age. At the age of 35, the contribution level rises to 19.5% while tax relief is limited to 20%. Making the step-change at 40 requires 23% of earnings above the level for full tax relief.

Figure 3.10: Lifetime poverty profiles (the effect of step-change requalification through a full-time higher education course ending at 30, 35, 40, 45 and 50 [private stakehoder pension fund with no commission on annuity])

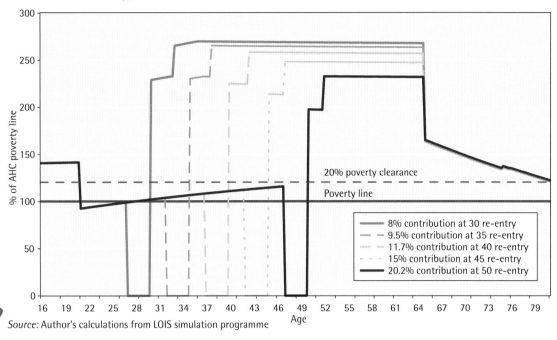

Source: Author's calculations from LOIS simulation programme

Figure 3.11: Lifetime poverty profile: Mr Meager (the effect of step-change requalification through a full-time higher education course ending at 30, 35 and 40 [private non-stakeholder pension fund with current market annuity])

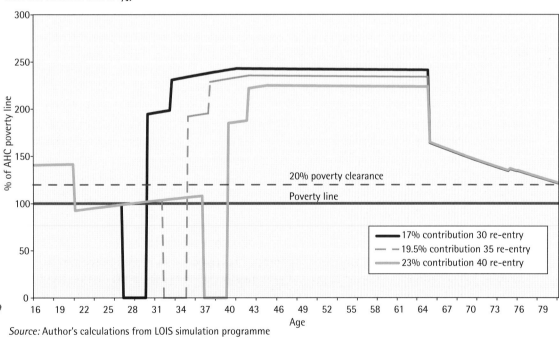

Source: Author's calculations from LOIS simulation programme

We therefore have a policy dilemma if we want to raise earnings at some point in a low-paid lifetime and equalise pension outcomes. First, the value of pensions varies so much between occupational final salary and money purchase schemes that the opportunities to save are even more severely constrained than for Mr Modal – partly because of the differences in value, but also partly due to the lateness of the step-change in lifetime earnings. Additionally, the available opportunity to save in money purchase pension schemes should, for any rational saver, be taken-up regulated stakeholder schemes, despite the fact that their income at the point of joining the scheme is way above that of the target group for such pensions. However, information on targeting is purely on a point in time definition of earnings – irrespective of what previous earnings or previous savings behaviour has been. Last, the link between pension outcomes and contribution levels means that the more expensive forms of contribution constrain other ways in which Mr Meager is able to equalise his lifetime opportunities with Mr Modal – through housing options in particular.

These costs of joining pension schemes mean that if we were to now join these results to consideration of buying a home then there are four important interacting factors:

- *House prices* will have risen faster than earnings, meaning that affordability worsens over the lifetime without regard to other income commitments such as pension contributions. This means that …
- *disposable income levels* and saving capacity while earning, alongside paying contributions to a pension, may mean that average earnings are not high enough to take out a mortgage later in life.
- *Mortgage loan time limits* also restrict opportunities to buy – the later in life one takes out a mortgage the sooner it has to be paid back – 15 or 20 rather than 25 years. But the ability to obtain a loan is also affected by …
- *the level of pension outcomes* we have set these in a consistent way to that of Mr Modal in Chapter 2 – in order to obtain a 20% poverty clearance throughout retirement. But, if mortgage repayment commitments continued into retirement then there would need to be higher pensions, or, alternatively, one would have to convince a mortgage lender that future pension income was sufficient to continue to make mortgage repayments during retirement.

It is thus probable that Mr Meager may be able to make up on one dimension of life chance inequality with Mr Modal – either pensions or home ownership – but it would be very difficult to see him reducing the gaps on both unless he was lucky enough to be able to join a pension that gave good returns for fairly low contributions. If current trends continue and employers continue to increasingly refuse access to defined benefit occupational schemes for new entrants then this does not look likely.

Improving job progression

Mr Meager has an alternative route out of lifetime poverty if he increases his earnings through job progression. His earnings capacity can grow over time as his experience on the job is rewarded, through promotion and through job mobility. If we consider such earnings progression it may be that low pay merely reflects an early stage of the lifetime earning profile rather than a long flat trajectory as previously considered. How quickly must earnings progress to escape the lifetime consequences of low pay?

Figure 3.12 shows two assumptions of earnings progression – a 5% progression every five years and a faster 5% progression every two years. These estimates make no allowance for differences over the working life from age-related factors (see previous discussion in **Box 2.1**). We begin earnings progression from the age of 25 and for the sake of argument

Figure 3.12: Lifetime poverty profile: Mr Meager (the effect of earnings progression on AHC income aged 16-64 [state contributions only])

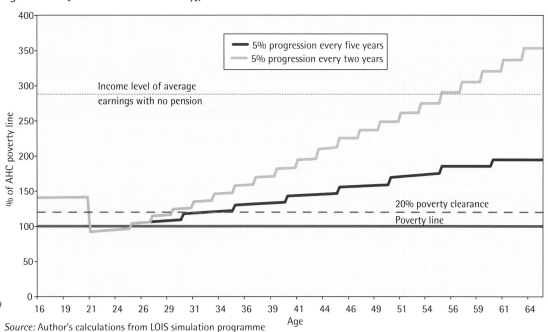

Source: Author's calculations from LOIS simulation programme

maintain it throughout the whole working life until the age of 64. The lower level of earnings progression – of 5% earnings growth every five years (additional to underlying earnings inflation at the average) brings AHC income above the 20% poverty clearance level at the age of 34 but income never reaches the level of AHC income that would result from average constant hourly pay. At its highest, this brings income to a 94% poverty clearance. On the other hand, an earnings progression factor of 5% every two years brings AHC income to a 20% poverty clearance at age 30 and then crosses the average wage marker level at age 55.

When we bring forward the lessons already learned from the analysis of step-changes in income, it is obvious that the lower rate of increase (5% every 5 years) is not sufficient for most private pension provision. However, **Figure 3.13** shows that the higher earnings progression (5% every 2 years) makes both contribution levels to pensions and pension outcomes more sensible. We have only simulated the defined benefit occupational pension and the 'best value' defined contribution money purchase scheme, and we only start simulating contributions when income passes a 20% poverty clearance. The defined benefit occupational pension gives rise to a pension that gives a 154% poverty clearance at the age of 65 and a 90% poverty clearance at death at the age of 81. The best value money purchase scheme to achieve a 20% poverty clearance requires a 9.6% contribution rate.

Low-paid lifetimes: conclusions and summary

Low pay seriously prejudices lifetime income and lifetime opportunities. While current tax credits and benefits appear to currently offer the low paid some limited guarantee about poverty while in work, they are not set up to maintain relative living standards in the medium to long term. As current assumptions stand, the low paid will pay more tax over their lifetime (fiscal drag) for a declining level of state support. However, such limited support is only for those aged 25 or over and the risk of low pay for younger people is high and has potential lifetime consequences, especially if incentives to save for retirement are sought to be taken up earlier and further down the income distribution.

Figure 3.13: Lifetime poverty profile: Mr Meager (5% earnings progression every two years from age 25 to 64 [state pension, best and worst value private pension and occupational pension])

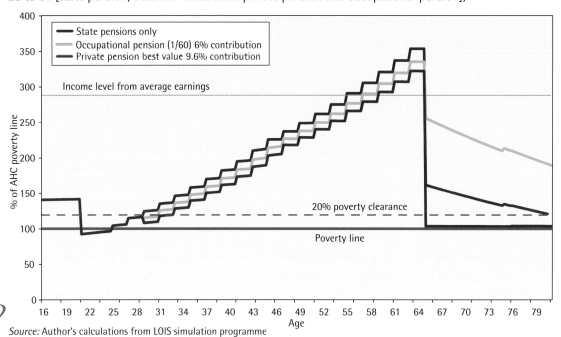

Source: Author's calculations from LOIS simulation programme

When we compare low-paid lifetimes to average-paid lifetimes, we can identify factors that additionally constrain opportunities and widen inequalities. First, the issue of tenure where renting raises the likelihood of lifetime poverty due to rent levels and rent inflation for the low paid. Second, compared to owner-occupation, renters' relative income gap widens over the lifetime as mortgage interest costs are at nominal sums fixed from the date of the loan (subject to interest rate variation). Third, the ability to gain access to pension provision is constrained not only by income and affordability but also because of income profiles over the lifetime, and we have explored the ability to change these profiles through step-changes and incremental earnings progression.

The results from step-changes and from incremental earnings progression suggest strongly that one-off interventions to raise income up to the average are *potentially* more effective in reducing inequalities in life chances and to bring lifetime opportunities up to the average for single people. The rate of earnings progression has to be high and there is a need to start early in the working life to bring earnings up to average levels. While it would be a mistake to say that it is sometimes 'too late' to intervene in a low-paid lifetime, the later such intervention is left the more serious are the constraints in opportunities to save or own a home, making a large impact on lifetime income profiles. However, these opportunities are not equal in value – private money purchase pensions require higher contributions for lower outcomes when compared to occupational defined benefit schemes. The type and value of a private money purchase pension scheme also matters a lot and regulated funds aimed at low to medium earners misses lifetime earnings profiles where such levels are not constant.

The opportunity trap

Equalising access to opportunities is an important policy approach for lifetime disadvantage, but our simulations suggest that too much reliance on such an approach is potentially naïve. There are constraints on reducing lifetime differences and equalising life chances that grow as the lifetime progresses. The gap between average and low-paid lifetimes can be bridged, but evidence suggests that this takes a substantial change in earnings at a point in the lifetime that is not 'too late'. There is a phenomenon where either the type of opportunity either fades or disappears (such as entering owner-occupation) or the terms of the opportunity mean high costs for fairly low outcomes. Where low cost and high outcome results are available they are often not available to those currently excluded by not already pension scheme members.

If we are to progress with policy based on an approach of offering opportunities we may also have to revise our thinking to realise that such offers are not equally available to be taken up and not designed to give equal value. Indeed, we suggest that there needs to be an awareness of potential lifetime *opportunity traps*. This concept may sound like an oxymoron because 'opportunities' are usually seen as the opposite of traps. An opportunity trap can exist where it is either too late or too costly to take up an opportunity – to be excluded or trapped out of opportunity – or where taking up an opportunity has either no or only a marginal impact on lifetime income profiles – to take up an opportunity and still be trapped.

Mr Meager's opportunity traps are potentially several: as a low earner he does not have access to pensions and owner-occupation, he is trapped out of opportunity. If he invests in his qualifications and skills and brings his earnings up to average levels he is still not assured that his opportunity profile is optimal – he takes up the opportunity and is still trapped. In this latter meaning, his choices of pension may be constrained – denied access to best value he may take up a poor value money purchase pension – limiting both his disposable income during his working life and also not optimising his income in retirement. All of these risks increase as he ages and the prospects of an opportunity trap grow more likely.

We develop and expand the idea of opportunity traps in the next chapter to look at long durations of constrained access to opportunities as well as events and life trajectories that block or thwart them.

Family lifetimes

There's nothing surer
The rich get rich and the poor get poorer
'Ain't we got fun' (song by Richard A. Whiting, Raymond Egan and Gus Kahn, 1921)

This chapter looks at children's potential effect on policy over our lifetimes. We limit discussion and analysis to couple families, leaving discussion of lone parents to Chapter 5. We address two main questions:

- What are the lifetime opportunities and risks of poverty for those who partner and have children, and how do these differ for low-paid and average-paid families?
- What can help low-paid families secure more opportunities and avoid poverty?

Discussion of pensions takes a back seat in this chapter as the major issues of pension policy and lifetime opportunities have been considered in Chapters 2 and 3. However, we do look at the potential *combined* effect of having children and saving for retirement in the latter part of the chapter.

Bringing children into our model lifetimes means making a range of assumptions about partnering and birth. The main assumptions for our model family lifetimes are given in **Box 4.1**.

Ms Middleton

Ms Middleton's model lifetime is very similar to Ms Modal's from Chapter 2. She stays on at school and goes into higher education and starts work at 21. At this point she lives alone and rents (at the same rent figures used for Ms Modal in Chapter 2) and earns average hourly pay for women, working 38 hours a week. She meets her partner, who earns average male hourly pay and also works 38 hours a week, and cohabits with him at the age of 25. They continue renting but save to buy a house after they have paid off their student loans, and this allows them to purchase a family-sized house at an average house price (today's average price of £155,627[15]) at the age of 28, in time for the birth of their first child when she is 28 and followed by their second child when she is 30.

Ms Middleton does not return to work until her youngest child reaches five and starts school, when she works 16 hours a week (at the same underlying hourly pay rate as previously, in other words, without suffering a pay penalty for being out of the labour market for five years, which many women do), and then increases her hours back up to 38 when the youngest child goes to secondary school. Pension assumptions are that both Ms Middleton and her partner have employment with an occupational defined benefit scheme as seen in the case of Mr and Ms Modal (6% contribution and 1/60 accrual rate).

---

[15] ONS (2003) *Housing statistics*, Table 571.

Box 4.1: Assumptions for model family lifetimes: Ms Middleton and Ms Lowe

Bringing partners and children into lifetime discussion and analysis increases the complexity of potential interactions over the lifetime – both between people and between policy elements. Again, we keep things as simple as possible by using model lifetimes that have the following characteristics:

- The model lifetimes follow two women, *Ms Middleton*, who has average earnings and *Ms Lowe*, who is low paid.
- They partner someone with exactly the same age and life expectancy. This makes the parallel stories of their lifetimes coincide and avoids the problem of survivorship – these can be the subject of future analysis.
- Their male partners have similar earnings levels allowing for gender pay differences.
- Earnings profiles are kept to linear average levels rising by average earnings growth (see Box 2.1).
- The legal status of the partnership is largely immaterial for policy. Marriage affects the right to pensions based on a spouse's NICs and gives rise to greater legal certainty on separation and survivorship. However, neither of these affects our couples and they have indeterminate status. We call them the Middletons and the Lowes.
- The age at partnering is held common between the Middletons and the Lowes at 25 years in order to provide maximum consistency and comparability on income levels alone.
- Both Ms Middleton and Ms Lowe have their first child at 28 and then a second child at 30. The current average age at birth of the first child is around 27-28 (*Social Trends*, 2003).
- Simulation of the presence of children in both families is stopped at 16 for a consistent measurement of children's effects on the lifetime. In fact, if children remained in non-advanced education until age 18 they would continue to be treated as children by the tax and benefit system and would receive Educational Maintenance Allowances from the age of 16, depending on their circumstances.

Figure 4.1 shows the income and taxes paid over the lifetime for Ms Middleton, both when she was single, up to the age of 25, and when she was one of a couple subsequently. The period of her lifetime when children were present was from the age of 28 through to 46. We have assumed for the sake of simplicity and consistency with low-paid families that children become 'independent' at 16 and cease to be included in the Middleton's direct tax credits and benefits. A more realistic assumption for average earners would be to continue children until their 19th birthday to represent them staying on at school or college post-16.

Figure 4.1 clearly shows the impact of dual earnings on net disposable income with highest levels of income occurring when both Middletons are working full time from ages 25 to 28 and from 41 to 65. Ms Middleton's interruption in earnings while the children are of pre-school age are clearly shown by the reduction of earnings at age 28 through to age 34. Earnings rise, first as she returns part-time at age 35 and then again as she moves to full-time employment at age 41. Her age at these points match with her youngest child's entry into primary and then secondary school. Offsetting these decreases in earnings are benefits – Child Benefit and Child Tax Credit – but **Figure 4.1** shows these are at levels that nowhere near compensate for the loss of earnings. Child Benefit is a relative value of 2.4% of average earnings at the birth of the first child and then rises to 3.8% at the birth of the second child. By the time the youngest child is 16, Child Benefit has fallen to 1.7%. Child Tax Credit starts at 3.1% of average earnings at the birth of the first child and then falls to 1.5% before the second child is born and then rises to 3.0% at the second birth before falling in relative value until it too is only 1.1% of average earnings by the time the youngest child is 16.

Figure 4.1: Model lifetime: Ms Middleton (lifetime income and tax profile)

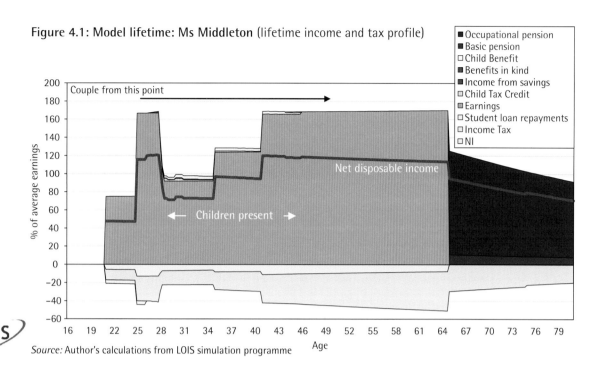

Source: Author's calculations from LOIS simulation programme

Box 4.2 gives details of these transfers for children. The main reason for their declining impact lies in the combination of benefit design, poverty measurement, up-rating and inflation. We take these issues in turn.

Benefit design

- *Basic assumption of flat rates as children age:* Child Benefit pays flat amounts as children age. Child Tax Credit pays higher rates for babies up to the age of one but otherwise pays flat amounts unrelated to children's age. Both Child Benefit and Child Tax Credit recognise the increased cost involved of having *any* children through the higher rate of Child Benefit for the first child and the family element of Child Tax Credit respectively.
- *Means-testing:* Child Tax Credit is means tested so that as earnings rise over time, entitlement falls. However, this effect is amplified by the next problem. Child Benefit is not means tested.
- *Up-rating and inflation:* only the child element of Child Tax Credit is committed to be up-rated with earnings (and only over the lifetime of the current Parliament). Child Benefit and the remaining components of Child Tax Credit are only up-rated with prices. This means that entitlement falls as earnings rise faster than prices and, as the relative poverty line rises with earnings, such benefits do not maintain their anti-poverty impact over time.

Poverty measurement

Measuring poverty in families and households uses an equivalence scale to make income relative to the number of people present (see **Box 2.5**). Children are taken to need less than an adult but as the child grows older their needs increase until they assume the same weight as an adult. The Equivalence Scale used throughout our analysis (the McClements AHC scale) increases child weights progressively. The scale proposed by the government to measure child poverty uses a higher average weight and then makes the jump to an adult weight at age 14 (the OECD scale).

Box: 4.2: Transfers for children

Maternity/paternity

Statutory Maternity Pay is available to all those who have been working for 16 weeks and paying NICs and who are pregnant and have either given birth or are within 11 weeks of giving birth. 90% of weekly earnings is given for first six weeks and then the minimum of £100 or 90% of earnings for 20 weeks. Statutory Paternity Pay at this latter rate is payable also for a maximum of two weeks. Maternity Allowance is payable at the second rate of Statutory Maternity Pay for many of those who fall out of this provision but are/have been working.

Child Benefit

Child Benefit is a non-means-tested benefit for every child aged under 16 and for those children aged 16-18 who are in non-advanced full-time education.

For the first/eldest child   £16.05 per week
For each other child   £10.75 per week

Child Tax Credit

Child Tax Credit is a means-tested refundable tax credit paid to the primary carer (usually the mother) both in and out of work for children that fit the Child Benefit entitlement rules. It is paid in addition to Child Benefit, which is ignored as income. Income is assessed on an annual basis on previous year's income. Full amounts of Child Tax Credit are shown below. The family element is paid once to all those with children and then each child receives a child element, which is higher for babies aged less than one. The combination of family and child elements are paid in full to all those with incomes less than the income threshold (£13,230 per annum) if Child Tax Credit is received on its own. If Child Tax Credit is received alongside Working Tax Credit then withdrawal of combined tax credits begins at £5,060 of income per annum. The taper is 37% above the income threshold.

Table 4.1: **Rates of Child Tax Credit 2003/04**

	Annual	**Weekly**
Family element	£545	£10.48
Child aged under one	£545	£10.48
Per child	£1,445	£27.79

Additionally, the family element is not withdrawn until income reaches £50,000 per annum.

Children with disabilities can receive a lower or higher additional element of Child Tax Credit.

Working Tax Credit: childcare costs

Working Tax Credit can include childcare costs to the weekly maximum of £135 for one child and £200 for two or more children. 70% of these costs can be covered by Working Tax Credit.

Up-rating and current profile of child transfers and in-work benefits

The child element of Child Tax Credit is up-rated with earnings but all other elements together with income thresholds for Working Tax Credit, Child Tax Credit and Child Benefits are up-rated with prices. Figure 4.2 shows how the current system works in current prices for a two-parent two-child family (children aged five and eight) who rent privately (at levels of rent and Council Tax of £132.90 and £17.90 respectively to match DWP Tax Benefit Model assumptions). Figure 4.2 shows how taxes and benefits change as earnings rise with increases in earnings based on increments of the National Minimum Wage at 38 hours a week.

Figure 4.2 shows Child Benefit paid continuously across the whole income range and other tax credits and benefits tapering out as income rises. Child Tax Credit continues high up into the earnings distribution with the basic child tax element only being withdrawn for earnings over five-and-a-half times the National Minimum Wage. However, the other elements of child credit

Figure 4.2: Child transfers and in-work benefits 2003/04 (couple with two children aged five and eight; single earner working at increments of National Minimum Wage 38 hours a week)

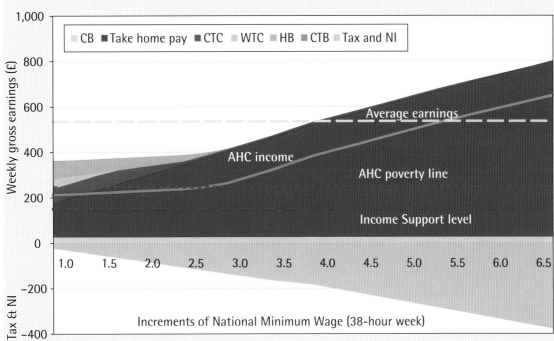

Notes: Rent £132.20; Council Tax £17.90.
Source: Author's calculations from DWP (2003b)

are withdrawn after Working Tax Credit entitlement ends at over one-and-a-half times the National Minimum Wage. Above this point Child Tax Credit is withdrawn and reverts to the basic element at over two-and-a-half times the National Minimum Wage. Housing Benefit continues up the earnings level depending on rent level – the higher the rent the higher up the earnings profile entitlement continues. In this example it ends at over three- and three-quarter times the National Minimum Wage.

Figure 4.2 also shows how AHC income rises relative to the poverty line. Income has a very shallow profile as earnings rise – due to tax, NICs and withdrawal of means-tested benefits. The combination of these tax and benefit tapers leads to high *marginal tax rates*, which are discussed further for the Ms Lowe model lifetime later in this chapter. For those on average earnings (single earners) then Figure 4.2 shows that Child Tax Credit would be paid at the basic amount – if, as in this illustration, no childcare element for Working Tax Credit was also in consideration.

Figure 4.3: Lifetime poverty profile: Ms Middleton

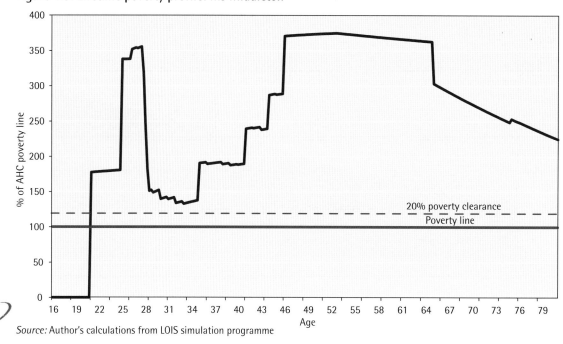

Source: Author's calculations from LOIS simulation programme

The effect of this, with income held nominally constant, is that families with children get poorer as their children age. The interaction of this effect with changing income for families is that benefits fall relative to the rising poverty line (from ageing children) because both Child Benefit and Child Tax Credit are eroding quickly relative to poverty in any case because the poverty line is additionally rising with earnings growth.

Figure 4.3 shows the lifetime poverty profile for Ms Middleton. The periods when two full-time average earners provide substantial levels of poverty clearance is clear. Even when there are children, full-time earnings provide a 139% poverty clearance when there are two children (at return to full-time work at age 41), and a 188% clearance when one child remains (at age 44). On the other hand, the greatest poverty risk arises from a combination of factors between the ages of 28 when the first child is born and 35 when Ms Middleton returns to work part time. Over this period, AHC income starts at a 52% poverty clearance and progressively worsens to a 38% clearance. Why has the Middleton's poverty risk grown over this period? There is a combination of lifetime, fiscal policy design and inflation factors that interact:

- first, the reliance on single earnings;
- second, the coincidence of this time with the earliest period of mortgage repayment and 'front-loaded' costs of the historically fixed debt at their worst;
- third, that the tax credits and child benefits decline in relative terms and thus in poverty support over time; and
- fourth, that measuring poverty gives greater equivalence weights to children as they grow older and as their consumption needs grow.

These mean that the Middleton children's needs grow but policy design means that the assistance paid to them does not grow with them.

There are a number of ways in which the Middletons could reduce the risk of their incomes falling so close to poverty. First, they could delay the birth of children until mortgage costs had reduced further in real and relative terms. Second, they could increase earnings – either through Ms Middleton returning to work earlier or through her partner working longer hours

Box 4.3: Assumptions for working with childcare

Combining work with looking after children brings with it a number of constraints based on the age and needs of the child and the relative costs of substituting caring to these needs to a third party and replacing up-paid work of the carer/mother with earned employment. We put forward three options for Ms Middleton.

Option 1: *Baseline assumption:* no work until both children reach primary school age when she returns to work, working a 16-hour week and then increases her hours to 38 when both children reach secondary school age.

Option 2: Ms Middleton brings forward her decision to return to part-time work to the point where the youngest child is two.

Option 3: Ms Middleton decides to return to work full time at the point where the youngest child is two.

These decisions have very different childcare consequences. To estimate the interaction of working and childcare we use cost assumptions taken from the Daycare Trust survey of childcare costs[16]:

Pre-school age:
- to work full time (38 hours) when children are of pre-school age we estimate childcare costs on the average £120 per week per child figure for childminding given by the Daycare Trust;
- to work part time (16 hours) we estimate childcare costs at £51.20 per week in current prices per child as a proportion of reported average costs of pre-school childminding.

Primary school age:
- to work full time we estimate costs, based on a 190-day school year and 20 days holiday entitlement for the parents, of combined after-school club of £35 per week and of holiday club at £65 per week;
- we estimate zero costs for part-time work for primary school aged children on the assumption that hours of work are arranged around school hours.

We simulate childcare costs rising at earnings inflation.

or going for promotion or some other form of earnings progression. If Ms Middleton chose to return to work earlier and even to return to work full time, then some of the gains from these earnings would be offset by childcare costs incurred. Ms Middleton's hourly pay rate, of around £11 in current prices, compare well to underlying hourly pay rates for childcare workers and childminding. It would be worthwhile as her earnings would be greater than the childcare costs (subject to tax and travel costs) and these would additionally be subsidised by increased Working Tax Credit and Child Tax Credit.

We re-simulate Ms Middleton's life using two scenarios that see her returning to work when her youngest child is aged two: first, returning to part-time work (16-hour week) and second, returning to work full time. More details about these assumptions and of other childcare assumptions are shown in **Box 4.3**.

---

[16] See Daycare Trust survey results, published annually at www.daycaretrust.org.uk. Childcare costs reported as paid by respondent families in the Family Resources Survey and other surveys tend to be lower than Daycare Trust surveys of providers' prices.

Figure 4.4: Lifetime poverty profile: Ms Middleton (changing work and childcare options)

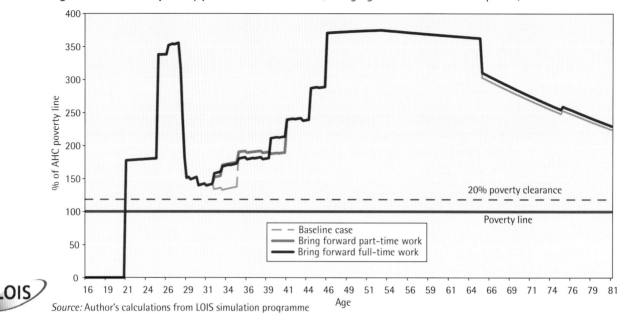

Source: Author's calculations from LOIS simulation programme

Figure 4.4 shows the effect of these alternative working patterns and childcare choices on the Middleton's income and poverty profile. The main impact of Ms Lowe returning to work earlier is to improve poverty clearance. Returning part time (16 hours) when her youngest child is two increases the Middleton's poverty clearance from 42% to 52% for the first year (when both children are pre-school) and then rises to 70% as her eldest child enters primary school. Returning directly to full-time work when the youngest child enters primary school yields no real increases in poverty clearance to returning part time because of the increased childcare costs until the eldest child leaves primary school and childcare costs reduce significantly (at age 39). At this point, poverty clearance increases to 111% if working full time and to 88% if working part time. Increasing work during childcaring years is also shown to improve later pension income. **Figure 4.4** shows a small increase in defined benefit pension from the additional years of work and earnings of Ms Middleton.

The combination of work and childcare appears to work for the Middletons, but timing and choice of part-time and full-time work is important – as are the levels of childcare costs. Overall, if Ms Middleton chooses to work and use childcare they can improve their overall living standards. Now let us turn to a low-paid family. How does low pay affect a similar family's living standards and opportunities?

Ms Lowe

Ms Lowe's lifetime has exactly the same demographic profile as Ms Middleton – she meets her partner and has children and has the same work history surrounding the births and child-rearing years as the Middletons. It is worth repeating these here to avoid readers having to hunt backwards in the text.

- Ms Lowe leaves work at the birth of her first child and does not return to work until her second child reaches five and starts school, when she works 16 hours a week (at the same underlying hourly pay rate as previously) and then increases her hours back up to 38 when the youngest child goes to secondary school.

Figure 4.5: The Lowes' lifetime income and tax profile

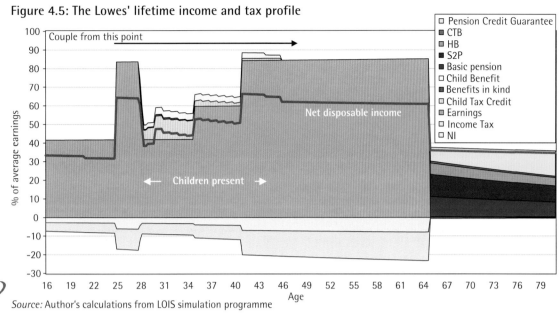

Source: Author's calculations from LOIS simulation programme

The big differences with the Middletons are that the Lowes' education and earning capacity resembles Mr Meager's – they never enter higher education and thus start work at 16. Ms Lowe and her partner are low paid, earning 0.6 of the male average hourly pay. They also rent throughout their lifetime and, in line with the assumptions previously outlined (see **Box 3.1** for a discussion on guidance rents for simulation) their rent rises and falls according to family composition and assumed spatial needs.

Figure 4.5 shows Ms Lowe's lifetime income components and disposable income over the lifetime. Neither her nor her partner have taken up alternative pension arrangements and rely on state pensions. The Lowes receive equal amounts of Child Benefit to the Middletons but much higher Child Tax Credits – at 8.1% of average earnings at the birth of the first child

Figure 4.6: Lifetime poverty profile: Ms Lowe

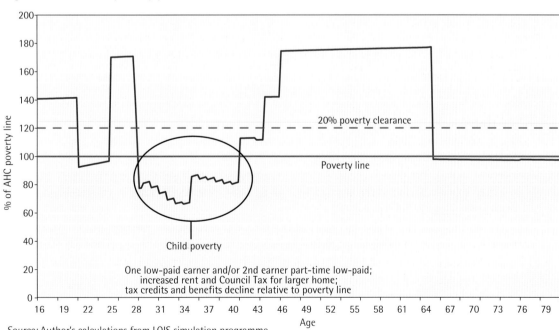

Source: Author's calculations from LOIS simulation programme

Box 4.4: Marginal tax rates

The current preferred term in government for marginal tax rates is the 'marginal deduction rate', but we follow the more common terminology and usage in the economics and policy literature.

The marginal rates of tax are based on the combination of the following:

Income tax rates:
10% on the first £1,960 of earnings above the personal allowance
22% on the subsequent band of earnings
40% on all earnings in the highest band

NICs (depending on non-contracted-out status):
11% for earnings above the primary threshold
1% additionally on earnings above the UEL

Housing Benefit/Council Tax Benefit:
65% taper on additional net-earnings (after tax and NICs) above Income Support level
20% taper on additional net-earnings (after tax and NICs) above Income Support level

Working Tax Credit:
37% taper on additional gross earnings above £96.78 per week
6.66% taper on additional gross earnings above £956.28 per week

Child Tax Credit:
37% taper on additional gross earnings above £253.03 per week where no Working Tax Credit is also in payment. Where Working Tax Credit also in payment the 37% taper begins at the point at which Working Tax Credit entitlement ends. Child Tax Credit is reduced to the minimum of the Family Credit element at an income level of £956.28 per week and subsequently a 6.66% taper on additional gross earnings above £956.28 per week.

Income Support and income-related Jobseeker's Allowance:
0% on income below set disregards
100% on income above set disregards.

Example (taken from DWP, 2003a, p 7)

For a standard rate tax payer (22%) also paying non-contracted-out NICs (11%) then the total marginal tax rate is 33%.

Working Tax Credit in payment is reduced at 37% (thus no additional reduction of Child Tax Credit)
Housing Benefit and Child Tax Benefit (65%+20%) x (1.00-0.33 -0.37) = 25.5%
Thus total marginal tax rate = 33%+37%+25.5% = 95.5%

In other words, an increase in earnings of £1 only results in a net increase in disposable income of 4.5p
Current estimations of marginal tax rates do not take into account contributions to non-state pensions. However, with Child Tax Credit eligibility and tapers rising up the earnings distribution to £50,000 per year and above, this is an omission that should be reconsidered.

Figure 4.7 shows the current system of benefits and tax credits for a family similar to the Lowes, where a single earner works for the National Minimum Wage for between 16 and 80 hours a

Figure 4.7: Benefits, tax credits and taxes for two-parent family with children (hours of work at National Minimum Wage, single earner)

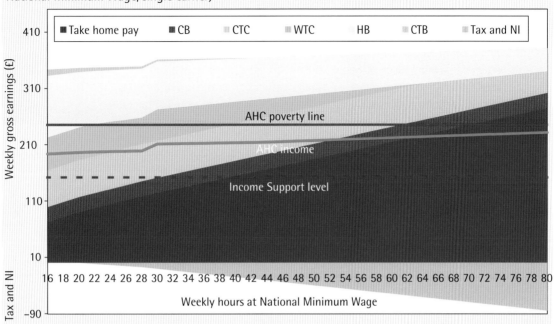

Source: Author's calculations from DWP (2003b)

week. (Working for more than 48 hours a week would be difficult in a single job because of working time restrictions.) The children in this example are aged five and eight and can be directly compared and this graph is consistent with and can be directly compared to Figure 4.2 above.

Figure 4.7 shows how difficult it is for families relying on the Minimum Wage to escape poverty. AHC income at 16 hours or more is always above Income Support levels, hence ensuring they are 'better off' in work than not working, but extra hours of work do not give the ability to escape from poverty – partly because of rent liability and Housing Benefit. Even at 80 hours there remains a 6% poverty gap.

Figure 4.8: Marginal tax rates for families with two children: five and eight (single earner's hours at National Minimum Wage [NMW] and multiples of Minimum Wage earning levels)

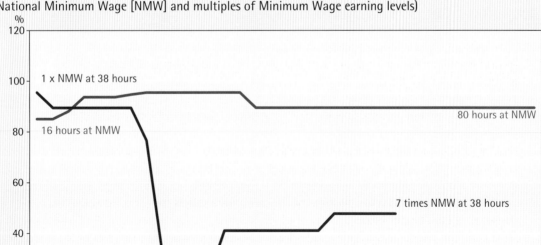

Source: Author's calculations from DWP (2003b)

Figure 4.8 shows the accompanying marginal tax rates for Figure 4.7 and compares them to those that arise from Figure 4.2. The red line shows the marginal tax rates for working 16 hours through to 80 hours a week at the Minimum Wage and show that the rates start at 85% and rise to 95.5% until dropping to 89% and remaining there. On the other hand, the blue line shows that at higher assumptions of earnings, such marginal tax rates fall. When working 38 hours a week at the National Minimum Wage marginal tax rates are 98%; these fall to 33% when only tax and NICs are taken from earnings before rising again as earnings enter the top rate for tax (41% marginal tax rate) and then rise to withdrawal of basic Child Tax Credit (48% marginal tax rate).

and rising to 12.6% at the birth of the second. However, both Child Benefit and Child Tax Credit fail to maintain their relative value as the children age – as previously discussed. This has serious repercussions for child poverty that can be seen in **Figure 4.5**.

Figure 4.6 shows that the Lowes have a similar but more serious income shock from having children to the Middletons. The Lowes, unlike the Middletons, drop directly into poverty on the birth of their first child while they rely on Mr Lowe's sole low-paid earnings. Worse still, their poverty worsens year on year as the poverty gap grows from 13% to 32% until Ms Lowe returns to work part time. This is due to the same combined effects that we saw with the Middletons – falling relative values of child benefits and tax credits and increasing needs of children as they age. However, it is also due to the fact that the Lowes' rent increases as they move to larger accommodation to meet their larger family. Help from Housing Benefit to afford this change is out of their reach because Housing Benefit entitlement has eroded over time and their income is increasingly above the entitlement threshold, which only rises with prices.

Ms Lowe's return to part-time work increases their income but only brings them to a 14% poverty gap. But continuing to work part time, their income falls behind and the Lowes fall further into poverty, increasing their poverty gap to 18% immediately before Ms Lowe starts to work full time. Full-time work does enable them to clear poverty and have a 13% poverty clearance but it is not until their first child leaves school that they have greater than a 20% poverty clearance (42%).

Escaping from poverty and marginal tax rates

How can the Lowes improve their income and avoid child poverty? Mr Lowe could, in theory, work more hours. However, when we remember the description of the interaction of tax, NICs, Working Tax Credit, Child Tax Credit and in-work benefits in **Box 4.2**, it leads to high marginal tax rates. **Box 4.4** gives more details about marginal tax rates and outlines how current tax and benefit tapers cumulate, concentrating on the low paid.

High marginal tax rates are one of the main disadvantages of means-tested delivery of in-work benefits and in the mid-1970s gave rise to the name *poverty trap* to describe the situation where people could not escape from low income because of high marginal tax rates. **Figure 4.7** in **Box 4.4** illustrates this phenomenon perfectly, with a single earner unable to lift the family income above the poverty line – even by working 80 hours a week (Piachaud and Field, 1971). However, within a lifetime perspective, the Lowes' case shows that there is the potential for such a trap to last over extended periods of the lifetime. The potential combinations of having children, childcare, paying rent and low pay and their interactions with tax credits and other in-work benefits mean that the Lowes will face not just high rates of marginal tax for a single year but for 16 years.

Figure 4.9: Model lifetime: Ms Lowe (effective marginal tax rates, single earner MTRs over the years of children being present)

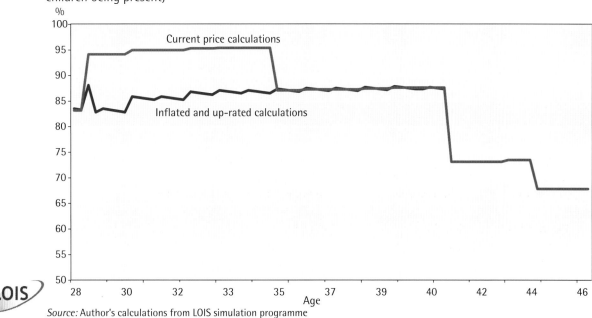

Source: Author's calculations from LOIS simulation programme

Figure 7.9 shows the Lowes' marginal tax rates over the period of their lifetime when they are children present (from the age of 28 to 45 inclusive), and are based on Mr Lowe working an additional hour. We show these marginal tax rates in both an up-rated and inflated lifetime as well as a lifetime lived entirely in current prices. The current price calculations give a clearer indication of what today's families with children face and match with the details given in **Box 4.4**. However, with up-rating and inflation over the lifetime, eligibility to means-tested benefits erodes and fiscal drag brings the low paid into higher rates of taxing and earnings growth, thus changing the profiles of marginal tax rates so that they are not entirely recognisable from today's system. **Figure 4.9** shows that under current price calculations the Lowes have a 95% marginal tax rate for a considerable period – linked to their receipt of Housing Benefit for that period. Marginal tax rates fall then to 87% for the remainder of the period and match the rate for marginal tax rates under inflated and up-rated calculations. Under inflated assumptions, marginal tax rates are lower overall because Housing Benefit does not feature as much. Additionally, Child Tax Credit and Working Tax Credit tapers give more fluctuation due to using last year's earnings as a reference point and also give rise to a spike in marginal tax rates at age 29. However, under both assumptions, the Lowes have marginal tax rates of 80% and over for *12 years* of their life.

This means that it is not only the rate of marginal tax but the potential *duration* of high marginal tax rates for long periods over the lifetime. If low pay is transitory then the risk is small, if high rent is transitory then likewise – but children are not transitory – they are around for at least 16 years. Long durations of high marginal tax rates in most cases build a further element to the idea of 'lifetime opportunity traps', first discussed in Chapter 3, and we will discuss this further later in this chapter.

Can the Lowes improve their poverty profile, even if constrained by high marginal tax rates? **Figure 4.10** shows how the Lowes' poverty profile changes if Ms Lowe duplicates the working and childcare options previously shown for Ms Middleton, that is, she brings forward her return to work when her youngest child is two and either works part time at that point or full time. The full assumptions and associated childcare costs are shown in **Box 4.2**. However, before we discuss the results from **Figure 4.10**, it is important to point out that low-paid workers like Ms Lowe *very rarely in fact combine formal paid childcare*

Figure 4.10: Lifetime poverty profile: Ms Lowe (changing work and childcare options)

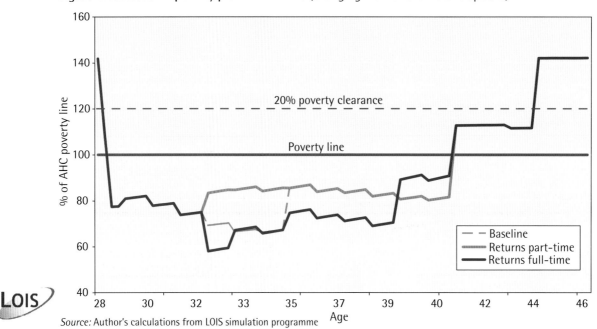

Source: Author's calculations from LOIS simulation programme

with low pay[17]. Readers should thus treat the hypothetical nature of simulations in **Figure 4.10** as a counterfactual case rather than illustrative of current empirical behaviour.

Figure 4.10 shows that neither full-time nor part-time work combined with childcare lifts the Lowes above the poverty line. It is not until both children are at secondary school and Ms Lowe can work full time without childcare costs that they have some poverty clearance. Part-time work with lower childcare works best. It lifts income and reduces the poverty gap from 25% to 17%. Full-time work actually reduces living standards because the simulation assumes that an element of childcare costs are above the levels for subsidy by Working Tax Credit and therefore Ms Lowe's earnings levels are not sufficient to make up the extra direct cost. However, once the eldest child is at secondary school and costs are reduced, then full-time work achieves a higher income than part time and reduces the poverty gap to 11% at that point. But it is worth repeating that these calculations do not reflect current usage of childcare in the same way as the Middletons. Low pay and formal childcare are a rare mix, part-time low pay and formal paid childcare almost never occurs.

So, the combination of low pay and children appears to mean a high risk of poverty and a high level of constraints on escaping poverty, both a poverty trap and a lifetime opportunity trap. As an alternative to Ms Lowe working and paying childcare, how high would Mr Lowe's income have to rise to escape poverty and ensure poverty clearance?

Figure 4.11 shows the effect on poverty of incrementing Mr Lowe's earnings by 50% intervals from the baseline as previously shown in **Figure 4.6**. Raising earnings by 50% alone does not lift the Lowes out of poverty until Ms Lowe also returns to work part time. A further 50% incremental increase not only raises income over the poverty line but also ensures a 20% poverty clearance for the whole of the time that children under 16 are in the family.

---

[17] For instance, changes to Housing Benefit disregards for childcare for low-paid families introduced in April 2004 were found to have little resulting impact on Housing Benefit spending as take-up of paid childcare was low in this group. (Our thanks to HM Treasury for discussion on this point.)

Figure 4.11: Lifetime poverty profile: Ms Lowe (raising first earner earnings by 50% increments)

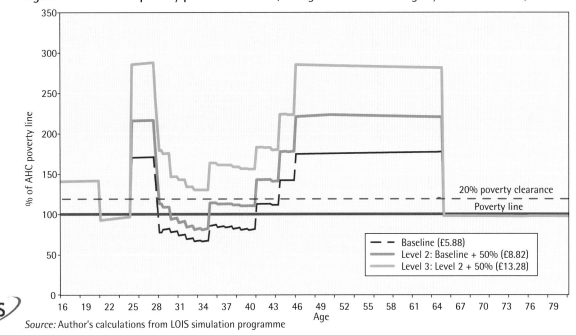

Source: Author's calculations from LOIS simulation programme

But as we see from the examples in **Figure 4.8**, raising income during the child-rearing years has done nothing to raise income in retirement, as the Lowes have still no private or occupational pension. At present, relying on state pensions and Pension Credit Guarantee, they have a retirement income around 2% below poverty (unlike the guarantee for single people at around 4% over poverty).

Now comes a real lifetime poverty dilemma. We know from Chapters 2 and 3 that contributing to pensions can have serious effects on current income. A contribution of 6% of earnings toward an occupational pension would represent best value – but where would that leave disposable income during child-rearing years? If we return to the assumptions shown in **Figure 4.8** and take the highest level of pay for Mr Lowe simulated by incremental increases of his earnings (two 50% increases), how would this be affected if this pay increase was also associated with joining a pension scheme? The higher assumed earnings level (£13.28) for Mr Lowe represents an annual salary of £26,240 per year and thus brings the Lowes fully into the mainstream of those identified by the government as being appropriate for private pension saving. Indeed, such a salary level is roughly at the top end of the target group for stakeholder pensions.

Figure 4.12 shows the outcomes of contributing 6% of earnings from the increased level of pay. We simulate two sets of pension to give a range of pension outcomes for the same contribution: an employer-run, defined benefit scheme and the 'worst value' private money purchase scheme running on non-stakeholder fund charges and on commercial annuity purchase (single life). We know from Chapters 2 and 3 that these two choices provide a wide difference in pension outcomes and **Figure 4.12** confirms this. The employer-defined benefit pension outcome, even for Mr Lowe only, provides a retirement with ample poverty clearance. However, the private money purchase scheme has much smaller levels of poverty clearance and the Lowes would rely on Pension Credit at some point in their

Figure 4.12: The lifetime poverty see-saw: The Lowes (Mr Lowe with enhanced earnings and pension choices)

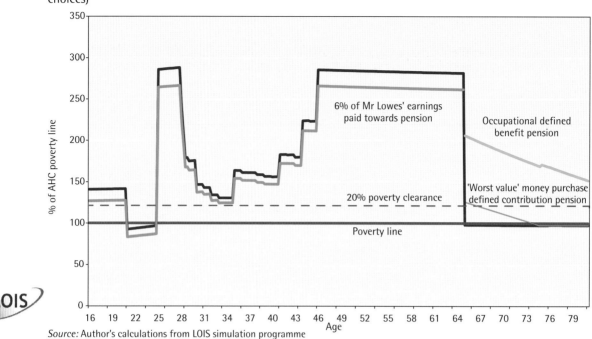

Source: Author's calculations from LOIS simulation programme

retirement[18]. To obtain a better outcome from the money purchase scheme they would have to contribute more than 6% of Mr Lowe's earnings, but if they did so then **Figure 4.12** shows that they would reduce their level of poverty clearance earlier in their lifetime when they had children. This means that, if they are to rely on a private money purchase pension, the Lowes are in a lifetime poverty dilemma that we call the *lifetime poverty see-saw*:

If they contribute more to their pension then their children's risk of poverty increases – the child-rearing years are at the bottom of the poverty see-saw.

Or

If they contribute little they can protect their children further against poverty but they themselves are very likely to be poor in retirement – the retirement years are at the bottom of the poverty see-saw.

This lifetime poverty see-saw is most prevalent for those with children, and is worsened by the combination of low to moderate earnings and the absence of a defined benefit occupational pension. If a family is low paid then their lifetime situation is a more 'simple' opportunity trap – they have too little earning capacity to obtain poverty clearance when they have children and in retirement. Low to moderate earners are more likely to be able to escape the opportunity trap but less likely to be able to balance the lifetime poverty see-saw.

---

[18] The estimation of after tax income for small entitlements of private pensions is difficult because of the interaction with Pension Credit and taxation under the current assumptions on up-rating. Small entitlements to 'Pension Credit – Savings Credit' occur alongside tax liability and until full 'Pension Credit – Guarantee Credit' comes into simulated entitlement, the estimated income outcomes are too unreliable, inconsistent and confusing to report. For this reason we have drawn an estimated line for the money purchase pension for illustrated purposes only. This ignores the perverse interactions of Pension Credit and tax but is based on the level of annuity purchased from the fund at age 65.

Family lifetimes: conclusions and summary

Having children increases the overall lifetime risk of poverty. Having children raises a family's need levels and constrains the ability to work of their parents – usually of the mother – for a period. A single-earner family with children will thus reduce poverty clearance for a couple on average earnings when they move from dual to single-earner status when the children are born and in their early years. The model lifetime based on a couple with average earnings, the Middletons, who additionally purchase their first home just before they have their first child and thus increase their need levels at that crucial time around the arrival of children, are still able to maintain levels of poverty clearance above 20%. However, model lifetimes based on low-paid couples, the Lowes, fall into poverty when they move to single-earner status and have children.

The risk of child poverty is increased by the design of benefits as they are flat rate and not up-rated with earnings. This means that children get poorer as they age because their increased needs are not met by increasing real income rises.

One of the main ways of reducing the risk of child poverty is by a quick return to two-earner status. This strategy increased poverty clearance for the Middletons, even when accompanied by childcare costs. However, for the low-paid Lowes, this strategy reduced poverty gaps but did not enable them to achieve poverty clearance. This demonstrated why low-paid parents tend currently not to use formal paid childcare. The Lowes were more able to improve their lifetime poverty profile by having higher earnings capacity – commanding a better wage rather than working more hours or both parents working.

Work incentive issues, however, are difficult as taxes and means-tested benefits interact to produce high marginal tax rates. While children are present in the household then marginal tax rates of over 80% can be the norm. Such long durations of high marginal tax rates leads to a new form of lifetime opportunity trap – where taking up the opportunity to work more provides no real benefit and does not allow low-paid families to climb out of poverty and achieve reasonable levels of poverty clearance.

The risk of childhood poverty means that those on low to medium earnings have great difficulty ensuring poverty clearance at both child-rearing and retirement stages of the lifetime. Saving for retirement while children are present will reduce poverty clearance merely to gain such poverty clearance later in life. Failing to do so reverses the lifetime poverty profile so that avoiding child poverty may lead to poverty in retirement. This dilemma is called the 'lifetime poverty see-saw'.

Lifetime risks

I claim not to have controlled events, but confess
plainly that events have controlled me. (Abraham Lincoln, Letter to Horace Creely,
1862)

Get today's solid ground out of yesterday's quicksand. (Mos Def, song, *Know that*)

So far, Chapters 2, 3 and 4 have looked at model lifetimes based on relatively straightforward profiles – earnings trajectories are mostly flat and the only interruptions to working life have been based on looking after children. In this chapter we change emphasis and look at events that are associated with a high likelihood of lifetime poverty. The events we examine are, first, unemployment, second, sickness and invalidity and third, lone parenthood. However, the impact of an event on lifetime poverty depends on when in the lifetime it occurs as well as the nature and severity of the risk event itself. Timing is important. Events that occur early in life can have potential scarring effects later on. For instance, youth unemployment has been shown to be detrimental to later employment (Gregg, 2001). Second, events later in life leave less opportunity to make amends or to redress potential lifetime impact and we have seen this in the idea of 'opportunity traps' discussed previously. Because timing is so important we also alter the underlying earnings assumptions in the model lifetimes in this chapter. We move away from flat linear assumptions about lifetime earnings and move towards age-related earnings profiles that reflect the labour market rewards for experience and skills and have a basic 'n-shape'– with pay lowest in youth, rising to its highest points in the forties and then slowly falling as skills and productivity are alleged to decline. Such an approach makes interpretation of underlying earnings profiles a little more difficult but clarifies and emphasises the importance of the timing of events when measuring their lifetime impact.

Figure 5.1 shows two earnings histories with the same underlying wage profile up to age 24. The green line shows the effect of having identical gaps of two years at three points in the working life – in the twenties when earnings are rising, in the late thirties when earnings peak and in the fifties when earnings are declining. We assume that these gaps are not used to improve earnings capacity and that in this first instance, using the green line, age-related earnings progression continues unaltered by the gap. Each identical gap has a different outcome on total lifetime income in nominal terms. We estimate this at just over a million pounds in today's prices (based on average hourly pay for a 38-hour week). So, the effect of a two-year gap between the ages of 24 and 26 is a 3.8% reduction in overall lifetime total earnings. But at 38 to 40 this same two-year gap reduces total lifetime earnings by 4.8% and at 54 to 56 by 4.2%. Thus timing definitely matters.

However, a gap usually leads to a wage penalty as people have lost experience and skills and have fallen behind those who remain in work. The **blue** line estimates the effect of the same gap for the same income profile up to 24 and then a two-year gap to 26. If this results in a 10% penalty (which we assume for the sake of argument is not later made up by earnings progression) then total lifetime income is reduced by 12.4%.

Figure 5.1: Age-adjusted lifetime earnings aged 16-64 with gaps and penalties

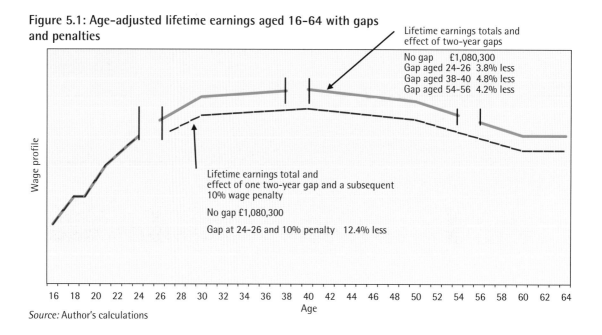

Source: Author's calculations

Such gaps and penalties are prevalent in women's earnings histories but also affect those with absences through unemployment and sickness (Joshi et al, 1996; Rake, 2000). We use model lifetimes incorporating such gaps and penalties throughout this chapter.

Mr Jobin: low-paid lifetime with unemployment

The risk of unemployment is not spread equally across the earnings distribution. The low paid are more likely to be unemployed. Indeed, Stewart has demonstrated that low pay is as powerful a predictor of future unemployment as unemployment itself and that there is thus a low-pay no-pay cycle (Stewart, 1999). How can we represent unemployment as a lifetime event? One approach would be to have a model lifetime cycling between low pay, even the National Minimum Wage, and periods of unemployment. This form of unemployment could well be mostly short-term periods between poorly paid jobs, with no single period of unemployment being seen as cyclical or leading 'long-term' unemployment, which in later life can be difficult to distinguish from early retirement. We opt instead to illustrate the effect of *single unemployment events* in our model lifetime analyses. We will discuss some aspects of other profiles as we proceed through this part of the chapter.

The model lifetime that incorporates unemployment is called Mr Jobin. He has a duplicate life to Mr Meager – always low paid and always single – except that he also suffers single periods of long-term unemployment of 18 months. Such unemployment can be seen as representing a macro-economic shock. We have two versions of Mr Jobin, one who suffers unemployment early in life and the other who suffers unemployment in his fifties.

Figure 5.2 shows the taxes and benefits for Mr Jobin's lifetime if he experiences his unemployment when he is 27. The earnings profile differs from those shown in earlier chapters as earnings are simulated as age-related, which gives rise to the overall curved profile. However, the National Minimum Wage level prevents earnings being curved down below that level and thus there are flat periods of earnings at the earliest and latest portions of the earnings history. Even on low pay the impact of the period of unemployment is marked. Disposable income falls from 30% of average earnings to 21%. While unemployed, Mr Jobin receives contributory Jobseeker's Allowance for the first six months and then moves on to income-related Jobseeker's Allowance. **Box 5.1** gives details of the current

Figure 5.2: Model lifetime: Mr Jobin (lifetime income and tax profile unemployed at 27 for 18 months)

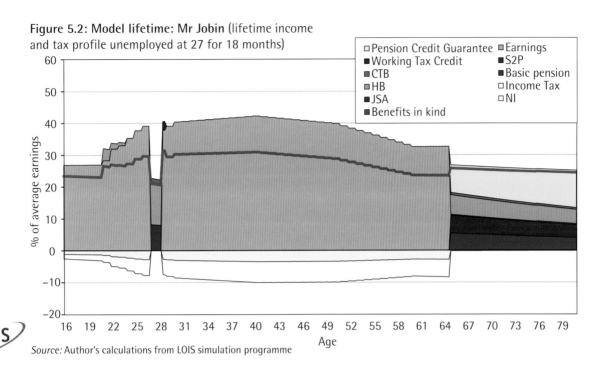

Source: Author's calculations from LOIS simulation programme

LOIS

system of unemployment benefits. He also receives 100% of his rent and Council Tax in Housing and Council Tax Benefits. On his return to work he receives Working Tax Credit. This eligibility does not arise directly from earnings levels, which are estimated to suffer a 10% penalty (see discussion above). Low pay – even at National Minimum Wage levels – would not qualify for Working Tax Credit because of the erosion of eligibility as earnings rise over time, as previously seen in Mr Meager's profile in Chapter 3. Eligibility for Mr Jobin arises from Working Tax Credit being based on annual estimates of income, and thus as his income is reduced to Jobseeker's Allowance levels, he qualifies for the first six months of returning to work on low pay.

The remainder of Mr Jobin's lifetime resembles a poorer version of Mr Meager – lower earnings levels and a retirement to state pensions and Pension Credit Guarantee.

Why is the income shock of unemployment so great, even for the low paid? Policy since the early 1980s has sought to ensure that incomes from out-of-work benefits are low enough to maintain incentives to work. The ratio of in-work to out-of-work income is called the out-of-work *replacement ratio*. Weekly rates of Jobseeker's Allowance are identical to basic rates for Income Support and were £54.65 for those aged 25 or more and £43.25 for the 18-24s in 2003/04. Jobseeker's Allowance is up-rated with prices. The payment of Housing Benefit and Child Tax Credit in addition to Jobseeker's Allowance enables rent and Council Tax to be paid but essentially disposable income is at basic Jobseeker's Allowance rates after housing costs.

The underlying trends in benefits and earnings outlined in **Box 5.1** help us understand Mr Jobin's experience of poverty resulting from unemployment over his lifetime. **Figure 5.4** shows the poverty line for Mr Jobin for two lifetime unemployment profiles:

- first, as previously discussed – for the period of 18 months when he is 27;
- second, for a period of 18 months when he is 50.

To aid comparison, **Figure 5.4** also shows the line for no unemployment on the same age-related earnings profile.

Box 5.1: Benefits for unemployment and the replacement ratio

Jobseeker's Allowance

Contributory Jobseeker's Allowance for the first six months of unemployment is paid to those who have previously paid NICs. The contribution rules are two-fold and complex but in simple terms are:

- in one tax year of earnings that are 25 times the lower earnings limit for NICs; and,
- in two years prior to being unemployed have paid NICs on earnings equal to 50 times the lower earnings limit.

For people without NICs, then, income-related Jobseeker's Allowance is available at exactly the same rates. To qualify for both forms of Jobseeker's Allowance you must not be of pension age or in work, be capable of work, not a student in higher education, be 'available for work', 'actively seeking work' and have signed a jobseeking agreement with the DWP and attend the Jobcentre Plus office.

Jobseeker's Allowance lasts for a maximum of 26 weeks.

What are the underlying lifetime incentives to work for Mr Jobin and others like him who are low paid and unemployed? Figure 5.3 shows disposable income from the ages of 18 through to 60 on the National Minimum Wage (38 hours a week) and from Jobseeker's Allowance. On the right-hand scale is the resulting replacement ratio, showing that Jobseeker's Allowance starts as a replacement ratio of just over 30%, dips when the National Minimum Wage rises at 22 to 27% and then rises again at 25 when higher rates of Jobseeker's Allowance come into effect to 30%. From that point until the age of 60 the replacement ratio falls to 17%. The downward profile of the replacement rate over the working life reflects the different assumptions for up-rating benefits (by prices) compared to earnings growth. We assume that the National Minimum Wage grows with average earnings growth, in fact the Low Pay Commission have argued that in the short to medium term it should rise slightly ahead of earnings growth (LPC, 2003). This profile ensures steadily improving work incentives but at the same time means that incomes when out of work for the unemployed fall further below the poverty line – shown additionally in Figure 5.3. Currently relying on Jobseeker's Allowance as a single person gives rise to an approximate 60% poverty gap and this will grow over the lifetime to 80%.

Figure 5.3: Incomes from Jobseeker's Allowance (JSA) and National Minimum Wage (replacement ratios and poverty ages 18-60)

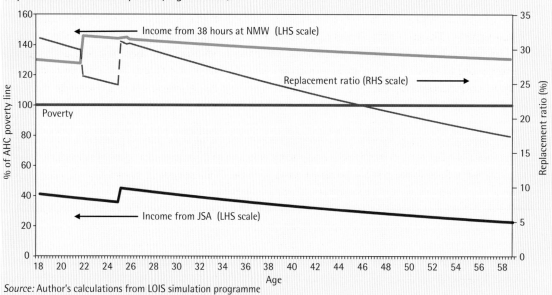

Source: Author's calculations from LOIS simulation programme

Figure 5.4: Lifetime poverty profile: Mr Jobin (effect of 18 months unemployment at either age 27 or 50)

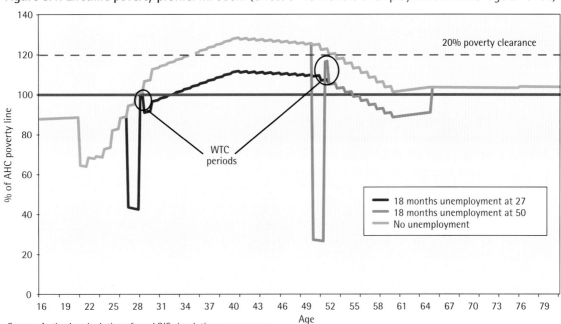

Source: Author's calculations from LOIS simulation programme

Figure 5.4 is based on the same assumptions for housing costs as were previously discussed for Mr Meager. Mr Jobin thus lives in his parents' home until 21, then rents, and the interaction of low earnings in youth and the effect of leaving home and paying rent is clearly shown at that point. In reality it is very unlikely that Mr Jobin could afford even the low assumed rent (£85 in current prices) that we have given. The main focus of results for **Figure 5.4** relate to the effects of unemployment on the subsequent lifetime poverty profile. Being unemployed at age 27 gives rise to a huge decrease in income at a point of time, a lifetime poverty shock. Income falls from a 10% poverty gap to a 57% gap. On returning to work, a wage penalty of 10% is assumed and Working Tax Credit is paid in addition for the first six months back at work under the Working Tax Credit annual income assumptions described above. The short-term income impact of Working Tax Credit is to bring income up to the poverty line, but after this it falls back after Working Tax Credit ends to a 10% poverty gap before rising again due to age-related earnings increases.

Unemployment at 50 leads to a much bigger lifetime poverty shock. Income falls very dramatically from a 24% poverty clearance to a 73% poverty gap. Returning to work is at a wage penalty and we have assumed this to mean that wages are at National Minimum Wage levels. Because Mr Jobin is over 50 he receives short-term Working Tax Credit supplementation of his earnings under the return to work rules but there is no underlying entitlement to Working Tax Credit – even on National Minimum Wage – as eligibility has eroded due to price up-rating alongside earnings growth. The result is that Working Tax Credit brings income up to the poverty line for six months and then ends and income falls back to a 16% poverty gap.

Mr Jobin's retirement outcomes are the same under both assumptions and under the assumption that he suffers no unemployment at all. This raises the issue about long-term versus short-term incentives to work. Replacement ratios for unemployment are very high and ensure throughout the lifetime that Mr Jobin is better off in work than unemployed. But it comes to a point in the lifetime where short-term and long-term incentives are more difficult to reconcile. Yes, Mr Jobin returns to work after 50 and does so and is better off – but he is still poor. He additionally gets no income gain in retirement from such work. If he is myopic he will not realise, if not, then the incentives become less clear-cut. Why work

38 hours a week when it makes no difference to where you will be in two or five or ten years' time? We return to this discussion in Chapter 6.

Low-paid lifetimes with incapacity

Evidence additionally shows that the risk of leaving employment after becoming sick and in some way less able to work is associated with age. Those aged 45 and over are most at risk (Burchardt, 2003). For these reasons we construct a model lifetime of a male single person who is low paid and who becomes incapacitated, Mr Hales – Mr Jobin's doppelganger. Mr Hales thus has a low-paid age-related earnings profile, rents throughout his lifetime after leaving the parental home at 21.

Figure 5.5: Model lifetime: Mr Hales (lifetime income and tax profile: working 20 hours a week from 45)

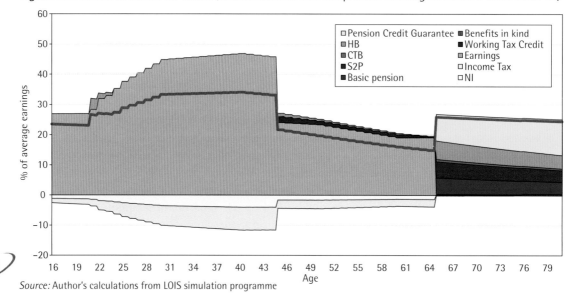

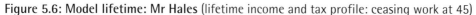

Source: Author's calculations from LOIS simulation programme

Figure 5.6: Model lifetime: Mr Hales (lifetime income and tax profile: ceasing work at 45)

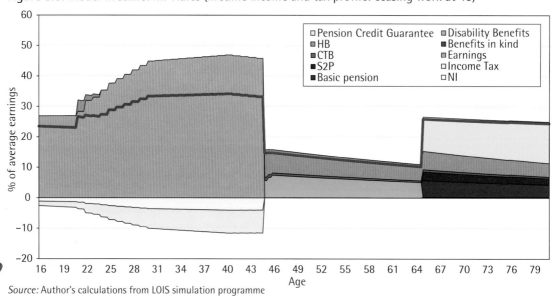

Source: Author's calculations from LOIS simulation programme

Box 5.2: Benefits for incapacity and disability

Statutory Sick Pay

Statutory Sick Pay is paid through the pay packet as a minimum level of sick pay for those employed and earning more than the lower earning limit (£77 a week in 2003/04) and of working age (16 to 64). It is paid for a maximum period of 28 weeks and was £64.35 a week in 2003/04.

Incapacity Benefit

Incapacity Benefit is a contributory benefit and relies on previous payment of NICs unless the individual became incapacitated before they were aged 20. Three years of contributions are needed prior to qualification[19]. Incapacity Benefit is usually paid at 29 weeks of a period of incapacity at three rates in 2003/04 rates:

£54.40 if paid for first 28 weeks of incapacity instead of Statutory Sick Pay.
£64.35 for weeks 29 to 52 of incapacity.
£72.15 from the 53rd week of incapacity (additionally for all those terminally ill).
Incapacity for work is established through an *own occupation* test for the first 28 weeks of claim and then moves to a *personal capability assessment* test.

Disability Living Allowance and Attendance Allowance

Disability Living Allowance and Attendance Allowance are non-contributory non-means-tested benefits paid on qualification through a medical test. They are designed to meet the additional costs encountered through having a disability – for instance, mobility and care costs. Disability Living Allowance is paid to those who are aged under 65 and Attendance Allowance is paid to those aged 65 and over.

Both Disability Living Allowance and Attendance Allowance give care components that have a qualifying condition that the claimant requires from another person frequent attention in connection with bodily functions or continual supervision to avoid substantial danger to themselves or others. There are three rates:

Lower rate Disability Living Allowance (£15.15)
Middle rate Disability Living Allowance and lower rate Attendance Allowance (£38.30)
Higher rate Attendance Allowance or Disability Living Allowance (£57.20)

In addition, Disability Living Allowance has a mobility component at two rates:

Higher rate (£39.95)
Lower rate (£15.15)

Entitlement to Attendance Allowance/Disability Living Allowance triggers entitlement to higher awards of Income Support, Housing Benefit and Council Tax Benefit. Middle and higher rates of Attendance Allowance/Disability Living Allowance give rise to entitlement for the carer of Carer's Allowance if they are not also in full-time employment and give regular and substantial care.

Working Tax Credit and disability elements

Additional Working Tax Credit is available for those whose disability puts them at a disadvantage in getting a job. The test of qualifying disability is quite wide and in addition it covers periods of habilitation and rehabilitation. Additionally, there is passported entitlement for those who currently receive Disability Living Allowance, previously received Incapacity Benefit at higher rate or disability premiums in Income Support, Housing Benefit or Council Tax Benefit.

The disability element of Working Tax Credit adds a further £2,040 per annum (£39.23 per week).

---

[19] For precise contributory rules, see Tolleys (2003) or CPAG (2003).

Mr Hales becomes ill when he is 45. We explore several different versions of what could occur after this point. **Figure 5.5** shows what would occur if he lowered his hours to 20 hours a week and continued working. **Figure 5.6** shows what would occur if he never worked again.

Continuing to work gives rise to Working Tax Credit in addition to his lower earnings as Working Tax Credit has additional generosity through additional elements of tax credit called disability elements. Housing Benefit would also be paid, again due to additional elements present in both Income Support and Housing Benefit called 'disability premiums'. Box 5.2 gives an overview of all disability and incapacity-related benefits and tax credits. Mr Hales's disposable income after tax falls from 33% of average earnings in work to 20% and then falls as the age-related profile declines.

Leaving work would give rise to receiving Incapacity Benefit, paid in the first instance at short-term rates and then at higher long-term rates. Mr Hales's disposable income falls from 33% of average earnings at 45 to just 16% at the highest relative level of Incapacity Benefit payment, when he first qualifies for the long-term rate. Income from Incapacity Benefit then falls relative to average earnings as benefits are only up-rated with prices.

How do these different responses by Mr Hales to ill-health at 45 affect lifetime poverty? Answering such a question depends on how poverty is affected by illness and disability. We have already explained how poverty is measured and the assumptions (see **Box 2.5**) but the issue of disability raises further important issues about how to reflect disability needs when measuring poverty. It is unquestionable that disability brings with it additional needs and costs. Indeed, there are benefits designed to meet such additional costs – Disability Living Allowance for instance, as described in **Box 5.2**. However, poverty is measured by keeping the needs of different households consistently equivalent. How should income be thus adjusted to reflect such needs? One method is to alter the equivalence scale and if we do so, by increasing needs by the stipulated 10% suggested by the DWP in the Households Below Average Income series (2003b), then we impose a rigid reflection of needs that does not alter if incapacity or disability worsens. It does not seem sensible to adopt a position where a severely disabled person needing continual attention is treated equally to another who is entirely self-reliant, for instance.

An alternative approach, adopted here, is to ignore 'extra costs' benefits such as Disability Living Allowance in income totals and use the normal equivalence scales. This at least does not add different levels of income components but only uses a single deflator to compensate. However, this is a compromise and we join others (Burchardt and Zaidi, 2003) in recommending a more thorough review of how disability is treated in poverty measurement. Our approach also leads us to make some distinctions in the treatment of benefits and tax credits and to award the system more coherence than actually exists in practice. Our assumptions are shown in **Box 5.3**.

Figure 5.7 shows the poverty profiles that result from Mr Hales's two options after he becomes ill. He is better off remaining in work but still has a substantial lifetime poverty shock. Despite Working Tax Credit and Housing Benefit his reduced earnings bring his income from a 27% poverty clearance down to a 33% poverty gap. If he stops work then his income falls to a 57% poverty gap. Either way his income declines for the remainder of his life before he qualifies for a pension at 65. At this point Pension Credit Guarantee income levels mean that he is far better off in retirement than he was at any time since his illness.

But so far we have shown Mr Hales's condition as stable – neither improving nor deteriorating over time. What difference would a worsening condition make? **Figure 5.8** shows a revised working assumption where Mr Hales continues to work 20 hours until 50

Box 5.3: Assumptions on disability in poverty measurement

Our approach is to try to take out the 'additional cost' elements of the benefit system that reflect disability. This adjustment thus theoretically makes the incomes of disabled and non-disabled claimants equal by ignoring Disability Living Allowance and Attendance Allowance, which are specifically designed to meet additional costs that would in a more thorough equivalisation of income be adjusted to zero. We therefore ignore all Disability Living Allowance and Attendance Allowance in income when calculating poverty. However, as Disability Living Allowances are trigger benefits for additional Income Support, Housing Benefit and Council Tax Benefit it is not possible to completely adjust for the additional income that arises from entitlement to Disability Living Allowance and Attendance Allowance. This is because other entitlements such as Incapacity Benefit also trigger some of these additional elements of means-tested benefits and Incapacity Benefit is not an 'extra cost' benefit.

We do not adjust the disability components of Working Tax Credit as this assistance is not designed to provide extra costs but to increase the earnings capacity of those with impairment.

Figure 5.7: Lifetime poverty profile: Mr Hales (effect of incapacity at 45: working 20 hours or leaving work)

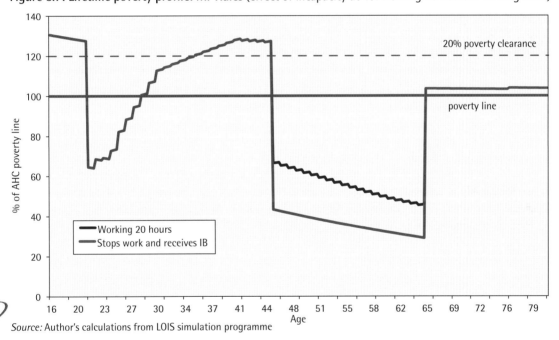

Source: Author's calculations from LOIS simulation programme

but then is forced to leave work as his condition worsens. Indeed it worsens to the point that he receives Disability Living Allowance at a low rate for mobility and care needs. This additional work period adds little in itself to underlying income out of work – adding nothing to the value of Incapacity Benefit and nothing to his later pension income. The only difference is that income falls to Incapacity Benefit levels five years later and that his qualification for Disability Living Allowance raises his notional disposable income while out of work to 17.5% of average earnings whereas it would be 16% above if relying on Incapacity Benefit alone. However, as we have already pointed out, to call this gain from Disability Living Allowance a rise in disposable income would miss the point that it is designed to cover his additional costs of being disabled. Alternatively, if Mr Hales had left work and his condition deteriorated in the same way then he could also have received Disability Living Allowance to assist him with the extra costs.

Figure 5.8: Model lifetime: Mr Hales (lifetime income and tax profile: ill from 45 ceasing work at 50)

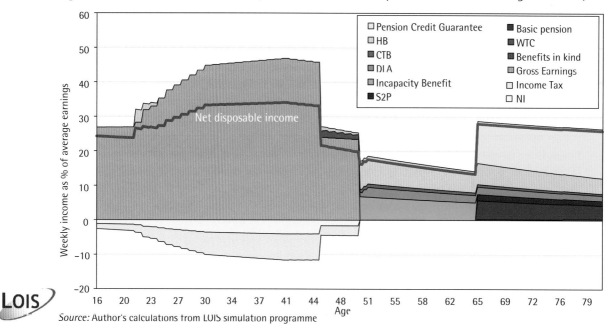

Source: Author's calculations from LOIS simulation programme

A further and final scenario is that Mr Hales recovers his health sufficiently to return to work full time at 50. We can assume that earnings suffer no penalty at return to full time as Mr Hales has maintained his skills and experience by remaining at work. **Figure 5.9** shows the lifetime poverty profiles of the following three scenarios:

- of a worsening condition that means that 20 hours work ends at 50 with Disability Living Allowance and Incapacity Benefit;
- of a worsening condition that means that, while remaining out of work, benefits are increased by Disability Living Allowance;
- of an improving condition where return to full-time work is possible at 50.

Figure 5.9: Lifetime poverty profile: Mr Hales (effect of incapacity at 45: working 20 hours or leaving

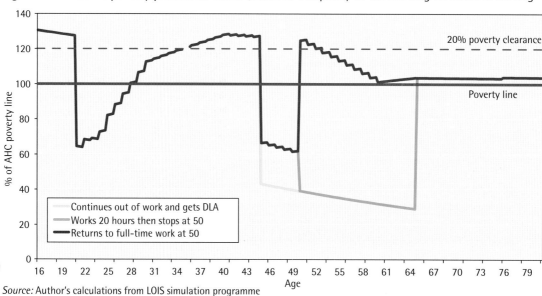

Source: Author's calculations from LOIS simulation programme

Only the option of a return to full-time work brings Mr Hales above the poverty line. His poverty profile out of work is the same whether he works further years and struggles on at work or not. Indeed, with Disability Living Allowance income disregarded to keep poverty measurement constant to needs, his out-of-work income is exactly the same as we saw previously in **Figure 5.7**. Of course, without any changes to pension assumptions, and there are few that can be made for someone with this level of low pay, then his poverty profile in retirement is unchanged across all scenarios.

Let us return to the issue of long-term and short-term work incentives discussed for Mr Jobin. Mr Hales has similar dilemmas regarding retirement income but also has only short-term incentives to remain in work. Yes, his income is much higher in work, whether 20 hours or returning full time to work. But these scenarios are based on the best profiles of illness and disability. If Mr Hales cannot work then there is little in the way of income security.

Lone parenthood

Our last model in this chapter explores the risk of lone parenthood. Lone parents are very varied in circumstances and life histories and our model lifetime, Ms Singleton, is designed to take forward what we have already learned from Chapter 4 by looking at separation. Partnership breakdown following soon after the birth of a child is a fairly common mode of entry into lone parenthood. Ms Singleton has an identical lifetime to Ms Lowe (see Chapter 4). This means that Ms Singleton leaves the parental home at 21 and partners at 25 and has her child at 28 but six months after the birth, her relationship ends and she becomes a lone parent. What impact does this make on her lifetime experience of poverty?

Our basic assumption for Ms Singleton is that she does not work after the departure of her partner until her child reaches school age, when she works part time 16 hours a week but suffers a 10% pay penalty. She then goes into full-time work when her child reaches secondary school age. **Figure 5.10** shows the resulting income components over the lifetime and her disposable income.

Figure 5.10: Model lifetime: Ms Singleton (lifetime income and tax profile)

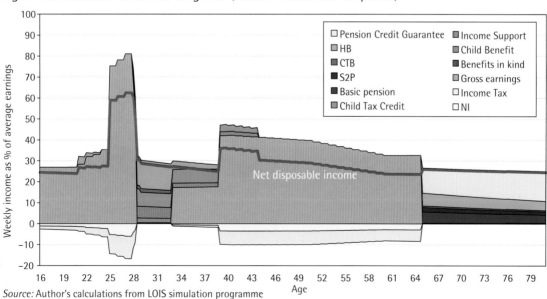

Source: Author's calculations from LOIS simulation programme

Becoming a lone parent results in a large income shock – the loss of a partner's full-time earnings and their replacement with Income Support. Disposable income falls from 60% to 30% of average earnings. Her income package out of work consists of Child Benefit, Child Tax Credit, Income Support and Housing and Council Tax Benefits. Returning to work part time does not increase her disposable income. This is a very surprising result, as the operation of the system today would ensure that there was a substantial gain to part-time work. The reason for this gain not appearing in our calculations is the relative erosion of Working Tax Credit and Child Tax Credit over time. Basically, this means that in less than 18 years time, the current assumptions for ensuring that work pays for lone parents will no longer stand up, a worrying future when child poverty targets are set to abolish child poverty within 15 years.

Returning to full-time work does substantially increase disposable income from 25% to 35% of average earnings. But once the child reaches 16 and Ms Singleton is no longer a lone parent, her income falls back to 30% of average earnings.

However, a further potential source of income is maintenance paid by her ex-partner, and **Figure 5.11** shows Ms Singleton's lifetime poverty profile with and without maintenance. We have calculated maintenance on the basis that her ex-partner has the same earnings profile as Mr Meager (age-adjusted). The lifetime poverty shock of entry into lone parenthood is stark, but mostly results from Ms Singleton stopping work and moving to a single-earner family with a child (see previous discussion of the Lowe family). Substantial levels of child poverty are present until she works full time. At the point of separation, six months after the birth, the resulting decrease in income increases the poverty gap from 20% to 25% only. If Ms Singleton continues not to receive maintenance then her poverty gap increases up to the point of entry into full-time work when it jumps from a 46% poverty gap to only 5%. However, maintenance makes a difference at the margin – reducing poverty gaps by around four percentage points until she enters part-time work at which point it reduces the poverty gap to 30%, a ten percentage point increase compared to no maintenance. Maintenance also ensures a 14% poverty clearance at the point of working full time.

Figure 5.11: Lifetime poverty profile: Ms Singleton (effects of receiving maintenance)

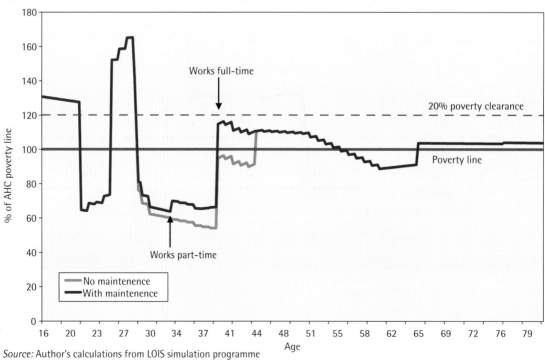

Source: Author's calculations from LOIS simulation programme

But neither part-time work nor maintenance solves child poverty. What is actually needed is higher earnings. We have seen from the Lowes in Chapter 4 that increasing hours of low-paid work through childcare makes little impact on poverty gaps for a two-earner couple, so there will be a similar or lesser impact for a lone parent. We will not repeat such analysis here. The only seeming way to radically improve Ms Singleton's life is either to increase her earnings capacity or to have her re-partner. **Figure 5.12** demonstrates the effect of re-partnering at age 35, after two years back in part-time work. Her former partner would continue to pay maintenance for the child, irrespective of the fact that she has re-partnered and thus we show how a new partner would affect poverty both with and without maintenance.

Figure 5.12 shows that partnering leads to poverty clearance, even while Ms Singleton is still working part time. Without maintenance she obtains an 11% poverty clearance and with it it rises to 25%.

The alternative, of increasing Ms Singleton's earning capacity, is of course possible and we have explored the potential to bring low pay up to average pay levels in Chapter 3 and intervening in Mr Meager's life. The same basic assumptions apply and we will not repeat that analysis here. But, there is an added difficulty in intervening to re-qualify Ms Singleton: her child. If she was to enter higher education, as a substantial proportion of lone parents wish (LPC, 2003), it would have to fit alongside her full-time childcaring before primary school age or alternatively replace or accompany a return to part-time work. Even so, it could potentially mean extending periods of quite severe child poverty.

Figure 5.12: Lifetime poverty profile: Ms Singleton (effects of re-partnering at 35)

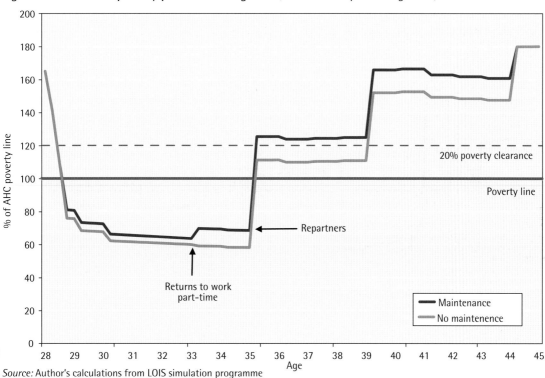

Source: Author's calculations from LOIS simulation programme

Lifetime risks: conclusions and summary

This chapter took model lifetime analysis a step forward by examining the effect that events can have on lifetime opportunities and poverty profiles. The events, of unemployment, sickness and incapacity and lone parenthood, are all associated with low pay and also act as amplifiers of low-paid disadvantage over the lifetime.

Unemployment during a low-paid lifetime is common and our model lifetime looked only at single instances of unemployment rather than cycles of low pay and no pay. Over the lifetime the difference between low pay and out of work unemployment support will grow – thus assuring high levels of replacement ratios but making poverty out of work a greater problem. Unemployment later in life and near retirement age appears to weaken incentives to return to work – even with very low benefit levels and high replacement ratios – because returning to work at low pay will have no effect on retirement income, which, if based on Pension Credit, may exceed living standards in low-paid work. There is thus a need to think of lifetime incentive issues as well as cross-sectional 'better off' assumptions that are based on simple transitions from benefits to work.

Such longer-term incentive issues and consideration of real incentives to work part time are explored further in the discussion of a model lifetime with illness and incapacity at the age of 45. Low-paid work is better rewarded due to in-work Working Tax Credit for disabled people but there is still little in lifetime incentives of a better future retirement income to make work worthwhile. Living standards are a big issue with poverty only avoided by full-time work. With benefits for disabled people only rising with prices, there is a growing problem to provide 'Security for those who can't work' (DSS, 1998, p iii), especially in their later life when likelihood of incapacity is highest.

Lone parenthood heightens the income shock of having children previously seen for couple families. Losing the main earner as well as having constraints on working through sole responsibility for children makes poverty very difficult to beat, even in work. Our calculations show that it is difficult to obtain poverty clearance if you are a low-paid lone parent – and most of them are both part time and low paid. The combination of maintenance and work works better but the best option to escape poverty is re-partnering.

Events that interrupt work thus make potential lifetime opportunity traps worse – they plunge low-paid people into significant levels of poverty as benefit levels out of work are very low. Escaping these when working with the constraints of children or disability is extremely difficult. Later in life, such events mean that returning to work for low pay provides an even poorer reward in lifetime terms as means-tested pension income is assured and will not normally alter through additional work effort. We know from Mr Meager and the Lowes in Chapters 3 and 4 that higher earnings capacity is what is mostly needed to escape lifetime opportunity traps. Current welfare-to-work programmes – the main response to such interrupting events in low-paid lifetimes – rarely provide this.

6

Conclusions

"The dead weight of low expectations,
the crushing belief that things cannot get better." (Tony Blair, June 1997, Aylsebury
Estate, Peckham)

Is a dream a lie if it don't come true
Or is it something worse? (Bruce Springsteen, 'The river')

The lifetime bench test

In our introduction we compared the lifetime profiling of the current tax and benefit regime
as similar to a bench test – similar to placing prototypes of aeroplanes or buildings in a wind
tunnel. Before reporting on the overall findings of this research and drawing conclusions,
it is worth reminding readers of the assumptions that underpin such bench-testing and the
limitations they carry forward to forming conclusions and recommendations for policy. First,
the lifetimes we have analysed are not based on a real sequence of events. We have tried
to replicate empirical evidence for modal and low-paid individuals in our simulations but
our model lifetimes are simplified hypothetical cases. Second, all of our lifetimes live under
all the current rules – no new policy is introduced to remedy weaknesses that are found,
and all of the compromises that today's policy makers have made to today's constraints are
extrapolated forward. Third, all of our lifetimes begin at the age of 16 in 2003/04 and this
means that inflation starts from the earliest period of the lifetime, and thus all findings on
inflation and up-rating report the worst possible scenario. Things would look different, but
not that different, if we started our lifetimes later, say at the age of 35 for instance, and if we
incorporated previous policy history and entitlements that had arisen prior to this starting
point.

Bearing all these caveats in mind, what does the lifetime analysis tell us?

A lifetime perspective on policy

A week is infamously a long time in politics and the idea of a lifetime policy approach raises
policy makers' planning horizons way, way further; even beyond the political cycle that
most adopt as a maximum. Fiscal policy tends to conform to an unwritten convention that
programmes of taxes and benefits will not bind future Parliaments. This convention locks in
short-termism. Advocates of the short-term policy view defend their position as 'democratic',
leaving the electoral cycle to decide whether today's decisions stand the test of time. This is
admirable but also builds in powerful messages of uncertainty to individuals who are trying
to plan their lives. It is also not consistent. Policy makers decide to build hospitals, schools
and roads, all of which have longer-lasting time horizons because they are infrastructure. At
the same time they ask us to plan our lives for the long term, to stop thinking myopically
– especially when it comes to saving for retirement. This does not fit well with short-term
fiscal policy. Perhaps we need to start thinking about lifetime fiscal infrastructure – longer-
term agreements or conventions to allow people to plan effectively and match their hopes

for the future more securely to today's decisions. Without any assurance of longevity we are left in the position that looks like the 1950s American automobile market – where shiny new cars were pre-rusted at the factory. Current fiscal policy is similarly destined to prematurely corrode.

Our approach using lifetime profiles of the current policy regime is one of the few ways of identifying such long-term structural weaknesses in fiscal policy and is both innovative and controversial. Through LOIS we have shown the power of 'joining up' analysis of long-term policy interventions such as pensions, savings, and investment in higher education with shorter-term current concerns about living standards, benefit rates, taxes, work incentives and poverty. We show that in the short term things roughly add up but the longer one looks ahead, the bigger the cracks.

What factors are of most concern in the medium to long-term?

Up-rating

It is less than 25 years ago that one fundamental piece of lifetime fiscal infrastructure was in place – the commitment to up-rating the majority of benefits and pensions with earnings growth. Such an approach gave an underlying certainty to lifetime relative living standards – an assured gradient for both protection against risk and on which to build savings and pension plans.

The evidence from previous chapters points to the following areas of concern.

Children and child poverty

Child Tax Credit and Child Benefit are the main fiscal instruments that help assure against child poverty. However, there is only a commitment to up-rate one element of Child Tax Credit (the child credit) with earnings and only for this Parliament. We have seen for both families on average (the Middletons) and low earnings (the Lowes) this approach means that the relative value of help for children declines. This means that the ability of these benefits to ensure that incomes clear a relative poverty line worsens. Given that child poverty targets are medium term in nature – over 20 years in total with currently around 15 years to go – and that the target includes a relative poverty measure, there is an underlying fiscal weakness in strategy.

This fundamental weakness interacts with two other factors discussed below: first, the inability to link parents' (adults of working age in the main) fiscal entitlement to any strategy of poverty prevention and second, flat rate child transfers.

Adults of working age

Both in-work and out-of-work benefits are only up-rated with prices. For in-work support, the lifetimes of Mr Meager and the Lowes showed how Working Tax Credit disappears for the low paid over time – even for those on the National Minimum Wage. This then affects the ability of low-paid parents of children to maintain living standards even where child transfers are relatively generous. It also affects the living standards of adults before and after they become parents and also in their ability to afford to save for retirement.

For those who have periods out of work then the coverage for unemployment, incapacity or lone parenthood will only rise with prices. Benefit rates already result in a 40% poverty gap and this will grow over time on current up-rating assumptions and is clearly unsustainable over the medium to long term. It also affects people with disabilities and thus means that income levels are a huge unaddressed issue across the board for security for those who cannot work. Short-term concerns about work incentives are an appropriate policy concern but replacement ratios will grow over time and the National Minimum Wage is due to rise with earnings over the short to medium term.

Turning to tax and National Insurance, then, up-rating with only prices means that people's inputs grow while parallel coverage declines in relative terms – basically they pay for more over time but get less back. Such fiscal drag is also unsustainable.

Pensioners

The long-term commitment to raise the Pension Credit Income Guarantee by earnings means it is only pensioners who have a commitment to a relative minimum income standard. However, this may raise the living standards for today's pensioners to poverty levels but means there are real problems for tomorrow's pensioners to beat this level of poverty assurance if they are currently not earning at average or above wages. We return to this below.

Up-rating thus affects the overall lifetime fiscal gradient – and there are two ways of thinking about the lifetime disadvantages of price up-rating: first, long-term investment and second, shorter-term income protection.

Investment decisions for pensions are hopefully based on a projection of what income is needed for retirement to protect living standards at a reasonable level. The basic pension has always been an underlying element on which other private investments are made. However, as basic state pension only rises with prices it is necessary to project forward a declining relative level of underlying support. You could think of this as trying to estimate the length of ladder required to climb up to a tower built several miles ahead, but with the land between you and the tower slowly tilting downwards. In order to know the length of ladder you need, you must estimate not just the known height of the tower above your head but the unknown difference in levels between your point and the ground around the tower.

With occupational defined benefit schemes this calculation is easier because you know your pension will be based on a proportion of your final earnings. However, with a funded personal pension that buys a weekly cash sum, it is more difficult to gauge how much cash fund and extra pension you will require. A projected pension of £50 a week on top of today's basic pension may seem like a lot of money and would give protection against poverty in today's prices – but would be way below poverty in 20-30 years time.

Shorter-term income protection becomes more difficult over time if out-of-work benefits do not rise alongside earnings. The risks of interruptions from work grow as people age but the relative protection from benefits falls alongside – leading to a problem of perceived equity because those with the worst chance of interruption are penalised by very high and growing relative falls in income when on benefits. Earnings, even at the National Minimum Wage will ensure they are better off in immediate terms but the choice between being poor in work or extremely poor out of work may mean that the huge lifetime income shock may blunt work incentives that are not short term and/or purely financial at the margins. We discuss this problem of short-term versus lifetime incentives below.

Responding to and measuring lifetime poverty

Poverty is an important element in measurement of policy effectiveness – both in the prevention of poverty as well as responding to it. Prevention and response over the lifetime echo Seebohm Rowntree's famous account of lifetime poverty risk in the first decade of the 20th century when he pointed to the risk of poverty coinciding with youth, having children and old age (1902). Those risks seem to be still with us, and especially so for the low paid, according to model lifetimes of Mr Meager and the Lowes. However, when we join up periods of high and low risk of poverty over the whole lifetime and think about prevention, then it becomes important not just to identify the durations and depth of poverty but also the duration and heights of *poverty clearance*. The term 'poverty clearance' is our own and has been adopted to enable us to look across the lifetime to see how income levels can potentially prevent poverty if saving or insurance can be made. If policy makers want individuals to take responsibility for their own lives and to make choices, then periods of poverty clearance enable saving for potential periods of poverty – especially in retirement. Thus the ability of lifetime income profiles to have periods of poverty clearance becomes crucial the more policy makers rely on intrapersonal redistribution of incomes over the lifetime rather than redistribution across the population.

This takes the debate on from aims that are merely about narrowing or closing poverty gaps at the times when they occur. It means, for instance, that raising earnings capacity of the low paid is a crucial lifetime anti-poverty strategy. But it also means that policies to prevent contemporary child poverty cannot just focus on children without also thinking about the lifecourse of their parents. Child poverty can be actually undermined if parents have to set aside considerable parts of income to save for their own retirement. We have illustrated this effect with the Lowe family, who, when we increased earnings from low to median earnings to solve child poverty, found themselves potentially put back in poverty once they additionally had to save for old age. We have called this problem the *lifetime poverty see-saw* – as the low paid are either protecting their children from poverty and ignoring their needs in retirement or vice versa.

Poverty over the lifetime also requires consistent measurement and we chose the HBAI after housing costs measure to ensure that we captured the differences between owner-occupation and renters over the lifecourse. Without such a measure that allows for housings costs there is an understatement of differences in disposable income; in particular between older households who own their homes outright and their peers who rent and also between them and their younger selves who are paying mortgage interest. However, we were faced with several difficulties in applying consistent poverty measures over the lifecourse. First, we developed a measure that took childcare costs from income to make childcare equal to rent and in order to discount payments of Working Tax Credit to cover childcare costs that would otherwise make families paying these and receiving help 'richer' than they actually are. Second, we also reduced income to take account of repayment of student loans in order to treat it as a deferred tax on higher education for graduates. Third, we had real problems in consistently considering the affects of disability over the lifetime, as we were unable to apply an equivalence scale that was linked to needs. Instead, we took the step of ignoring extra cost benefits – but this is a compromise because while such benefits do recognise additional needs and are paid at different rates according to needs, they also act as passports to other assistance which cannot be directly discounted. These difficulties reflect both shortcomings in available data at the time of writing and more structural problems in the approach to poverty measurement. The inclusion of measures that discount childcare costs in 2004 HBAI figures will be very welcome, while the unresolved issue of disability needs and the undercounting of poverty for disabled people continues and demands better attention.

Lifetime policy design

The current approach to policy separates children, working age and pensioner groups. This is no problem as long as there is the ability to reassemble such approaches into a set of sensible assumptions for the whole lifetime. If we take pension policy for instance, then targeting of stakeholder pensions on those with earnings within certain bands is not perhaps the best way of accurately predicting affordability. We have seen how the presence of children, housing costs and other factors make 'affordability' of private provision more complicated than simple earnings bands recognise.

Similarly, the design of child benefits and tax credits are flat rate and thus accept that children get poorer as they get older because all equivalence scales for poverty adjust need to children's age – whether incrementally or as a step-change at age 14. Of course, family income may rise as children get older and constraints on earnings lessen, but this does not alter the fact that the design of assistance for children and children's poverty measures are not optimally joined up. The design of Pension Credit Guarantee also gives different poverty coverage for singles and couples because the assumptions about equivalence are not matched between benefits and poverty measurement.

But some of the most worrying aspects of lifetime policy design lie in private pension provision. We have shown the huge advantages of regulation of administration costs and entry and exit charges on stakeholder pensions and these raise the value of saving considerably – and not just for the target group of moderate earners. However, helping to reduce the effectiveness of pension saving by regulating charges is only one step. We are still left with huge uncertainties about what pensions will result from these regulated funds. First, overall market risk underlying the investment may mean that funds at the point of retirement are not what was foreseen. The recent collapse of share prices following the dot-com boom demonstrates such volatility and is due to macro-economic factors outside of any individual's control, but can make or break any individual's plans for retirement. Second, not only is the amount of the final fund uncertain but also annuity rates are uncertain and contemporary experience shows this volatility as we have witnessed large falls in annuity rates from over 7% to under 5% in recent years. Third, there is little transparency about charges and commission in the purchase of annuities with the accumulated pension fund and there is a concern that regulation of accumulation may mean that financial providers take higher charges when converting that fund into a pension. Today's best annuity providers are additionally no guide to best practice or outcomes in the future.

The combination of these three unknowns builds in huge levels of what can be termed as 'unplannable uncertainty'. This operates alongside other factors that can be seen as uncertain but more plannable: the declining level of the state basic pension, which requires higher investment by individuals to maintain living standards in retirement; and future increased longevity. All in all, if we return to our image of trying to guess the length of ladder needed to enter the distant tower's window, we can extend the metaphor to say the following. First, that there is no certainty that the ladder will be built to a specified length when the time arises to enter the window – the price of wood may go up, the price of the carpenters may be higher and the supplier may take a bigger, unknown cut. Second, we also now realise that as well as the land leading up to the tower falling away we are also not so certain of how far away it is. So, even if we have a good idea of how high the window is above our head (that is, we have a clear idea of what living standard we are aiming for in retirement), our ability to reach it could be completely outside of our control – even if we take all reasonable steps to order and set aside funds to buy a ladder.

Axiomatic to future uncertainty is that today is more certain. Today's wants and needs are more pressing and the majority of messages from the market are about consuming now. Today's status goods are important social markers across the generations – increasing pressures on relative living standards for children, adults and older people. The government is thus right to try and make people more concerned about saving for retirement and to provide more information. But information and light regulation are probably not enough in themselves – there is a need to invest in what we have previously termed 'lifetime fiscal infrastructure'. This is not the place to start discussion of alternatives but the current combination of market risk and means testing is also not an entirely happy one. Items on LOIS' future research agenda will be to explore how far a greater reliance on contributory social insurance or compulsory private saving could more happily reconcile lifetime policy structures.

Lifetime incentives

Reconciling today's behaviour with later lifetime needs, however, also raises the issues of incentives. Currently these are purely thought about in cross-sectional terms as 'work incentives' or longer-term 'savings and retirement incentives'. Our lifetime approach joins these up.

Basic incentives to enter work are high if they are solely based on transitions into work at any single point of time. Such transition incentives grow over the lifetime for nearly all groups – in part because of declining levels of out-of-work benefits relative to the National Minimum Wage and earnings more generally. However, whether the low and declining level of out-of-work benefits is sustainable is a question we have raised previously. Incentives to work harder or longer hours are not so good. The growth in generosity and coverage of in-work tax credits, combined with means-tested benefits for rent, Council Tax, Income Tax and NICs mean that marginal tax rates are very high and at any point in time many low-paid people will face very high marginal tax rates and find themselves in the so-called poverty trap, working for very low returns – often an effective 10 pence in the pound on additional earnings if children are present. We have actually *underplayed* the issue of marginal tax rates in our model lifetimes because of the underlying problem of fiscal drag that brings even the low paid into the 40% tax bracket at the same time as entitlement to in-work benefits declines due to up-rating and inflation. This produces marginal tax rates that are difficult to reconcile with current assumptions and tables, and if we were to show lifetimes in current prices we could demonstrate even more clearly that many face high marginal tax rates for long portions of their working lives.

It is thus the *duration* as well as the *extent* of high marginal tax rates that raises potential concerns over the lifetime. Low-paid people with children are going to face 70p to 90p in the pound marginal tax rates for 16 years at least. If market rent levels rise ahead of earnings, the position worsens across the board for the low paid. Even for the moderately paid the issue of long durations on high marginal tax rates is potentially serious not only for the combination of Child Tax Credit with Income Tax and NICs but also for premium payments to pension providers. Indeed, it seems a strange convention not to include such payments into marginal tax rate calculations as private provision is encouraged further, and especially if compulsion is being considered for some groups.

Saving incentives are blunted for the poor by the inconsistency of treatment by benefits and tax credit rules. There are now three ways of calculating someone's savings levels and income from savings. At worst there are the savings cut-offs for entitlement to Income Support (higher for Housing Benefit and Council Tax Benefit) and treatment of tariff income, which are not up-rated at all. For lifetime risks this means that most of those who are unemployed, sick, disabled or lone parents during their working years are unwise to have more than £3,000 savings. Tax credits and pension credits have wider coverage and more generous tapers.

Longer-term incentives to save for retirement not only relate to the future treatment of savings but also in the effect of saving at all when Pension Credit Guarantee provides a guarantee that is difficult to beat if you are low paid and/or long-lived. The combination of the basic state pension and S2P is insufficient to beat the means test and opting out of S2P and subscribing to private pensions will be trying to fill a large and growing gap between pension credit entitlement and the dwindling state pension. We have also seen that, in the case of Mr Meager, intervention to raise lifetime poverty prospects means significant increases in earnings capacity early enough in the working life to make an impact on retirement. There is a time at which raising earnings to allow for contribution to private pensions is too late – it depends on income levels and, crucially, on the form and costs of pension provision. One of the outcomes of proper advice and information about the outcomes of retirement saving may mean that overcoming myopia will actually make clear when incentives to save for retirement are poor. This not only blunts savings incentives but can also blunt work incentives.

When we put these short-term and long-term incentives together we can see that there are combinations of events and times in people's lifetimes, especially if they are low paid, where there is little they can do to escape poverty – either contemporary poverty, being on the margins of poverty in old age or a combination of the two. This means that, as illustrated in Mr Hales's and Mr Jobin's model lifetimes, that illness and unemployment late in the working life can lead to a position where you can be better off in work but heading for a means-tested retirement nevertheless. If this is the case then it seems that weighing up the short-term gains of working when the long-term gains are zero is a crucial matter of concern.

Beating the opportunity trap

Current thinking about incentives is largely cross-sectional – we worry most about people's transitions between fixed states (usually out-of-work to in-work) rather than their trajectories. The idea of lifetime 'opportunity traps' more adequately illustrates how incentive problems can cumulate within a lifetime perspective. An opportunity trap is where the lifetime gain to a change in behaviour is minimal or zero. Examples are:

- taking up a private pension if retirement income is only marginally affected;
- taking a job if there is no ability to make overall life chances improve beyond moving from dire to moderate poverty in the short term;
- working longer hours, or potential second earners or partners starting work if marginal tax rates are high for years ahead is another example.

Beating such opportunity traps means policy could focus more on improvement of human capital and earning capacity early enough in the lifetime to make a difference. We have given some indications in Mr Meager's model lifetime that there are points at which it is, in theory, too late. Of course, we have to be careful in saying 'too late' too bluntly. In some cases people would be happy to extend their working life and defer retirement in order to make up ground. Additionally, we are not putting forward that such interventions are a waste of time – they can be perfectly justified in their own right at any age if personal growth and self-improvement are the sole aims of policy. But we know this is not the case and the efficiency and effectiveness of policy are the main drivers of policy design. This being so, it brings us full circle to the issue of how lifetime perspectives fit into short-term policy making.

Beating the opportunity trap means not only building more ladders out of poverty but investing in making overall lifetime gradients of opportunity less divergent. When we think about recent policy developments they have stressed the need for a developmental approach and equality of opportunity for children and young people. However, there comes a point in a lifetime that equality of opportunity is not a particularly helpful approach and more active interventions are required to make a lifetime impact. In many cases such interventions have moved forward greatly in recent years – employment programmes, for instance, with large investments occurring in improving quality and coverage of 'welfare-to-work' programmes. However, getting people into work is only one step of the process. We have shown in the model lifetimes, current fiscal policy design does not help in itself to ensure that they move on and earn more and beat the lifetime opportunity trap. Indeed, with fiscal drag and benefit entitlement falling as earnings rise, the low paid could end up paying more for lower levels of help with very uncertain lifetime outcomes. With current assumptions on benefit up-rating and inflation the low paid who fall out of work are on a downward escalator of relative income. Welfare-to-work programmes will make sure they do not keep still and thus stop them from falling faster and further, but they are really just getting people to run up the downward escalator. High marginal tax rates mean that they are unlikely to make any real progress upwards but are running to stand still at best. Only investing in higher earnings capacity can reverse the escalator.

Forthcoming evidence from the Job Advancement and Retention Programme should greatly assist thinking in this area and greater investment in in-work training and education could be part of the answer. But also a more nuanced approach to training and education out of work – trajectories and transitions could be better balanced as aims of active employment policy – especially as many of the participants are returning customers who have already been moved back to work before.

We started this report by saying that our position was as a 'critical friend' to the government and it is important to end with some recognition of the large short-term gains that have been made on poverty and worklessness over recent years. In the short term, Pension Credit will mean cash incomes at a level that many older pensioners and poorly paid workers have not experienced before, for instance. Child Tax Credit and Working Tax Credit will also raise families and poorly paid people out of poverty. But the longer-term prognosis is less rosy and policy makers across the political divide should think about how to put social policy back into a stronger lifetime perspective.

References

Baldwin, P. (1994) 'Beveridge in the Longue Durée', in J. Hills, J. Ditch and H. Glennerster (eds) *Beveridge and social security*, Oxford: Clarendon Press.

Bradshaw, J. and Finch, N. (2002) *A comparison of child benefit packages in 22 countries*, DWP Research Report 174, Leeds: Corporate Document Services.

Bradshaw, J., Ditch, J., Holmes, H. and Whiteford, P. (1993) *Support for children: A comparison of arrangements in fifteen countries*, DSS Research Report No 21, London: HMSO.

Bradshaw, J., Kennedy, S., Kilkey, M., Hutton, S., Corden, A., Eardley, T., Holmes, H. and Neale, J. (1996) *Policy and the employment of lone parents in 20 countries*, York: Social Policy Research Unit/European Observatory on National Family Policies.

Burchardt, T. (2003) *Employment retention and the onset of disability: Evidence from Labour Force Survey (LFS) longitudinal datasets*, DWP Inhouse Report No 109, London.

Burchardt, T. and Zaidi, A. (2003) *Comparing income when needs differ: Equivalisation for the extra costs of disability*, CASEPaper 64, London: Centre for Analysis of Social Exclusion, London School of Economics and Political Science.

CPAG (Child Poverty Action Group) (2003) *Welfare benefits and tax credits handbook 2003/2004* (5th edn), London: CPAG.

DfES (Department for Education and Skills) (2004) *Student loans and the question of debt*, London: DfES.

Ditch, J., Barnes, H., Bradshaw, J., Commaille, J. and Eardley, T. (1995) *European Observatory on National Family Policies: A synthesis of national family policies 1994*, York: Social Policy Research Unit.

DSS (Department of Social Security) (1998) *A new contract for welfare: Principles into practice*, Cm 4101, London: The Stationery Office.

DWP (Department for Work and Pensions) (1998) *A new contract for welfare: Partnership in pensions*, Cm 4179, London, The Stationery Office.

DWP (2002) *Simplicity, security and choice: Working and saving for retirement*, Cm 5677, London: The Stationery Office.

DWP (2003a) Tax Benefit Model Tables April 2003, Newcastle: DWP Information Centre.

DWP (2003b) *Households Below Average Income 1994/5-2001/02*, London: DWP.

DWP (2003c) *Measuring child poverty: Final conclusions*, London: DWP.

DWP (2004) *Households Below Average Income 2002/03*, London: DWP.

Eardley, T., Bradshaw, J., Ditch, J., Gough, I. and Whiteford, P. (1996a) *Social assistance schemes in OECD countries*, vol 1 Synthesis Report, DSS Research Report No 46, London: The Stationery Office.

Eardley, T., Bradshaw, J., Ditch, J., Gough, I. and Whiteford, P. (1996b) *Social assistance schemes in OECD countries*, vol 2 Country Reports, DSS Research Report No 47, London: The Stationery Office.

ESRC (Economic and Social Research Council) (2004) *Seven ages of man and woman: A look at life in the second Elizabethan era*, Swindon: ESRC.

Evans, M. and Falkingham, J. (1997) *Minimum pensions and safety nets in old age: A comparative analysis,* WSP 131, London: STICERD London School of Economics and Political Science.

Evans, M., Falkingham, J. and Rake, K. (1999) *Tightropes and tripwires: New Labour's proposals and means-testing in old age*, CASEPaper 23, London: CASE, London School of Economics and Political Science.

GAD (Government Actuary's Department) (2003) *Occupational pension schemes 2000: Eleventh survey by the Government Actuary*, London: GAD.

GAD (2004) *Interim life tables 2000-2002*, London: GAD.

Gregg, B. (2001) 'The impact of youth unemployment on adult unemployment in the NCDS', *Economic Journal*, vol 111, no 475, F626-653.

Johnson, P. (1999) 'The measurement of social policy convergence: the case of European public pension systems since 1950', *Journal of Social Policy*, vol 28, no 4.

Joshi, H., Davies, H. and Land, H. (1996) *The tale of Mrs Typical*, London: Family Policy Studies Centre.

Kilkey, M. (2000) *Lone mothers between paid work and care: The policy regime in twenty countries*, Aldershot: Ashgate.

LPC (Low Pay Commission) (2003) *The National Minimum Wage: Fourth Report of the Low Pay Commission, Building on success*, London: The Stationery Office.

MORI (2004) *Homeowners: Sons and daughters: A survey of parents who are owner-occupiers*, MORI/JRF, July.

NAPF (National Association of Pension Funds) (2003) NAPF *Annual Survey of Occupational Pension Schemes 2003: Main findings of Annual Survey 2003*, London: NAPF.

Piachaud, D. and Field, F. (1971) 'The poverty trap', *New Statesman*, 3 December.

Rake, K. (ed) (2000) *Women's income over the lifetime*, London: The Stationery Office.

Rake, K., Falkingham, J. and Evans, M. (2000) '21st century pensions – a partnership or a marriage to the means-test?', *Social Policy and Administration*, vol 34, no 3, pp 296-317.

Redmond, G., Sutherland, H. and Wilson, M. (1998) *The arithmetic of tax and social security reform: A user's guide to microsimulation methods and analysis*, Cambridge: Cambridge University Press.

Rowntree, B.S. (1902) *Poverty: A study of town life*, London: Nelson [reissued by The Policy Press/ Joseph Rowntree Foundation in 2000].

Stewart, M. (1999) 'Low pay in Britain', in P. Gregg and J. Wadsworth (eds) *The state of working Britain*, Manchester: Manchester University Press.

Tolleys (2003) *Social security and state benefits Issue 11*, London: Butterworths.

Ward, S. (2003a) *Your guide to pensions 2004: Planning ahead to boost retirement income* (10th edn), London: Age Concern.

Ward, S. (2003b) *Planning your pension: A TUC guide for everyone at work*, London: Kogan Page.

Appendix: Lifetime Opportunities and Incentives Simulation (LOIS)

Outline of LOIS

LOIS is a computer simulation programme that can model the British 2003/04 tax and benefit system over any hypothetical lifetime. The parameters of a lifetime are user defined and entered via a graphical user interface. Standardised model lifetimes can be developed using pre-set defined parameters. LOIS can operate on a current price basis by calculating lifetimes lived in today's prices but can also be set to different inflation and up-rating assumptions.

In-built formulae calculate a large variety of income and savings components over the lifetime, including benefits and tax credits, pensions, tax and National Insurance, savings and mortgage loan interest payments and house values. Outputs from the model are in a variety of forms:

- Final incomes can be reported according to several definitions for poverty measurement.
- Marginal tax rates can be calculated for all parts of the lifetime.
- Lifetime summaries of poverty, marginal tax rates, income and taxation can be produced and apportioned to periods of the lifetime.
- Graphical outputs are produced for income components, marginal tax rates and poverty profiles.

Hypothetical lifetime profiles and events

All lifetimes follow an individual and are single generation assumptions. Each lifetime begins at age 16 and has a maximum life span to the age of 95. The lifetime events that can be simulated are:

- Partnering and separation: a maximum limit of two partnerships throughout the lifetime has been set in order to keep programming and file sizes to manageable proportions.
- Children and stepchildren: a maximum of four children per adult, so a total of 12 children can be entered into the programme.
- Education levels for both adults: they can leave school with no qualifications or some qualifications less than A level; go on to further education and get A levels or other qualifications less than a degree; and they can go into higher education and get a degree-level qualification. Student loans can also be inputted for both the subject and a partner in order to simulate repayments once in work.

- Work details including hours worked, hourly pay and pension choice: work history for both adults can be interrupted with periods out of work due to child rearing, unemployment, disability or ill-health and education.
- Savings history can also be inputted with either weekly deposits or lump sum deposits and withdrawals simulated.
- Housing choices can be set to allow for any rent and owner-occupation can be simulated using a standard capital repayment mortgage.
- Childcare costs, either registered or unregistered, can be inputted for periods where there are children aged under 11 in the household and both parents are working.
- The new Child Trust Fund is included in LOIS, the amount given either £250 or £500 is selected, then amounts can be added to this initial amount until the child is 18, then they can either spend the total amount or choose to put it into a taxable or non-taxable savings account.
- At any point the subject or their partner can be made disabled and entitlement to Disability Living Allowance, Attendance Allowance or the disability element of the Working Tax Credit can be selected.
- Child maintenance payments either to the subject or partner or from the subject or partner can be simulated.

Our approach and how LOIS was built

LOIS is an Excel spreadsheet that contains 19 worksheets, within which formulae, macros and VBA (Visual Basic for Applications) coding runs the lifetime inputs through the formulae and produces outputs. VBA user forms have been used to enable the user to input the lifetime parameters. LOIS has an opening 'initial information' user form that asks for basic lifetime information needed for setting every lifetime, such as: name, gender, age at death, disability status, education level, age 16 event (that is, stay on at school, start first job or become unemployed), age left home and tenure, amount of Child Trust Fund received, amount put into the Child Trust Fund per year and the percentage of the Fund that was spent at age 18 when the young person can access the fund.

After setting this initial information the user can enter as many lifetime events as they wish. As shown in the report, the lifetimes can range from a fairly simple single lifetime, in the same job all their life retiring at age 65, to a more complicated family lifetime with separation and re-partnering, periods of unemployment and children.

Inflation and up-rating assumptions can be changed for each simulation. Indexed and inflated runs have a default set of parameters that mirror current government statements and practice on up-rating. These can be changed to re-simulate lifetimes under different combinations of inflation and up-rating assumptions. For instance, the difference of up-rating benefits and taxes by earnings rather than prices can be shown. There is also the potential to re-simulate the tax and benefit system on altered rates of allowances and benefits, although this has not been done to date and must be approached with great care as the potential interactions across the current system are difficult to anticipate and changing a single threshold or rate may have a variety of intended and unintended outcomes.

LOIS coverage of the policy system

LOIS can model means-tested benefits, non-means-tested or contributory benefits, statutory benefits and benefits in kind. The following shows all of the benefits that can be modelled with LOIS:

Means-tested benefits
Income Support
Income-based Jobseeker's Allowance
Housing Benefit
Council Tax Benefit
Working Tax Credit
Child Tax Credit
Pension Credit

Non-means-tested benefits
Child Benefit
Basic State Pension
State Secondary Pension
Contribution-based Jobseeker's Allowance
Incapacity Benefit
Attendance Allowance
Disabled Living Allowance
Carer's Allowance
Maternity Allowance

Statutory Benefits
Statutory Maternity Pay
Statutory Sick Pay

Benefits in kind
Welfare Foods
School Meals
TV licence
Winter Fuel Allowance
Xmas Bonus

Private and occupational pensions

LOIS can simulate pensions based on regular contributions from earnings to a variety of types of non-state pension. Defined benefit occupational pensions are based on a definition of final salary that can be defined by the user. Defined contribution benefits can be simulated using both employee and employer contributions into a savings fund and a specific rate of accumulation. Charges and commission can be set for such funds including stakeholder regulated options. Matured funds can then be simulated to purchase an annuity based on automated life expectancy, user-defined annuity rates and charge and commission assumptions. Tax relief to pensions is calculated automatically.

A website has been set up for LOIS to give further details and to present research and publications produced. The address is www.lois-web.org. E-mail lois@bath.ac.uk